A Daughter of the King

Gaining Confidence as a Child of God

TRACY HILL

© 2016 by Tracy Hill

All rights reserved. Except as provided by the Copyright Act no part of this publication may be reproduced, stored in a retrieval system or transmitted in any form or by any means without the prior written permission of the publisher.

Cover photographs copyright © Tracy Hill 2016. All rights reserved.

All Scripture quotations, unless otherwise indicated, are taken from the Holy Bible, New International Version®, NIV®. Copyright ©1973, 1978, 1984, 2011 by Biblica, Inc.™ Used by permission of Zondervan. All rights reserved worldwide. www.zondervan.com, The "NIV" and "New International Version" are trademarks registered in the United States Patent and Trademark Office by Biblica, Inc.™

Cover designs copyright © Camden Hill 2016. All rights reserved.

ISBN 978-0-9976913-0-6

Dedication

Dedicated to the precious women of Teen Challenge,

my dear friends at Club 31, and every woman who needs

the message of confidence that is found as a child of God.

Contents

Encouragement..1

Introduction...2

Chapter 1   You are Loved..4

Chapter 2   You are Forgiven and New...18

Chapter 3   You Belong..34

Chapter 4   You Matter..48

Chapter 5   You are Beautiful...62

Chapter 6   You Have Purpose..72

Chapter 7   You are Strong..86

Chapter 8   You are Royalty..104

Time to Soar..122

Leader Guide. 123

A Special Thanks...125

Getting to Know the Author..126

Additional Inspiration..127

Endorsements...128

My Encouragement to You

My hope is that you approach this study totally surrendered to what God wants to do in your life. Come before the Lord, asking Him to reveal His Truth to your heart by the power of the Holy Spirit. Come with an open heart, truly seeking to hear from the Lord, ready to be transformed by Him. I pray that these are not just words on a page, but that they come alive and stir something deep within you. Be prepared to let go of the former thoughts you have of yourself.

Only God can truly change your life, but you must be surrendered to what He wants to do and believe what He says about you.

Introduction

Am I loved? Can I ever get past my past? Do I belong? Do I matter? Am I beautiful? Does my life have purpose? Am I strong enough to get through this situation? These are the questions that wreak havoc on our minds. It is extremely important that we know without a doubt, God's Word answers every one of these questions with a LOUD, emphatic YES!

Unfortunately, we often allow ourselves to be weighed down with the heavy burden of insecurity. Some of us bear this burden all the time, while others of us pick it up and carry it every now and then. Still others instead wear the illusion of confidence— a confidence that is built on self, others, our accomplishments, or our possessions: things that will ultimately let us down. True confidence comes as we realize who we are in Christ.

God desperately wants you to know that you are loved, you are forgiven, you do belong, you do matter, you are beautiful, you have purpose, and you are strong. God's desire is for you to discover what it means to be truly confident as His beloved child, enjoying the rich blessings of your true identity which are found in Jesus Christ. The enemy wants you to believe otherwise, so you are going to learn to fight off the lies of insecurity with solid Truth. You are meant to live in confidence and victory as a Daughter of the King. You are royalty.

"I pray that out of His glorious riches He may strengthen you with power through His Spirit in your inner being, so that Christ may dwell in your hearts through faith." Ephesians 3:16-17

I have met enough women—and men, for that matter—to know that I am not the only one who has struggled with insecurity at some point in life. Chances are, this may be your struggle also. My hope is that through this study, you gain a new confidence that comes from your identity as a child of God. As you look to the Bible and begin to believe it as your foundation of truth, the thoughts in your mind will change to be filled with hope, peace, love, joy, and confidence—a confidence that causes you to stand a little taller, hold your head a little higher, walk with a new spring in your step, and face life head-on with the knowledge of your true identity.

To help reinforce the messages found in our study, I have made a series of short videos and podcasts to wrap up each chapter. *Begin* with the *introduction* video or podcast and then *follow up* each lesson with the *corresponding session*. **The videos can be found on my YouTube channel:** www.youtube.com/@beblessedandinspiredwithtracy/playlists

You can also listen on my Spotify podcast: Be Blessed and Inspired with Tracy Hill

It's also a wonderful way to share the message of *"A Daughter of the King"* with others.

QR Codes links for these sites are found on page 126.

"Satisfy us in the morning with your unfailing love, that we may sing for joy and be glad all our days."

Psalm 90:14

CHAPTER ONE

Love is the basic and essential foundation on which all our confidence and security is built.

No matter how old we are, no matter how many wrinkles or grey hairs we have, no matter how tough we act, deep inside our hearts there will always be a young, vulnerable girl who longs to be loved and cherished.

From the moment we are born, our heart's deepest longing is to be loved. Love is what keeps us alive; it fills us with hope and keeps us going. Sure, air, food, and water are vital to our survival, but, left alone without love and intimate connection, we will fail to fully thrive in life. Just knowing that we are loved makes all the difference in the world. I have a wonderful message for you: there is Someone who loves you more than you could ever imagine! You are on His heart and mind 24/7. He wants to have a personal relationship with you, to be the One you think of, the One you turn to, the One who fills you with joy and hope and confidence. He wants to go through life with you. God is the One who loves you so dearly.

Jeremiah 31:3, "I have loved you with an everlasting love; I have drawn you with loving kindness."

There is a space in your heart only God can fill, a void and emptiness He alone can satisfy. Come to Him and find the love that your heart longs for.

Deuteronomy 4:29, "But if from there you will seek the LORD your God, you will find Him if you search for Him with all your heart and all your soul."

From the beginning of time, you have captured Jesus' heart, and He has set out to capture yours. He thinks you are so lovely that He gave His life to have you as His own. No detail of your precious life is hidden from Him. Jesus wants to help you let go of the past and fully live in the present with Him. Knowing Jesus as Lord and Savior and believing His Promises to you, opens the door wide for wholeness and healing to enter in. His love has the power to change you from the inside out. To know and experience His love *personally* will fill your heart with a brand-new confidence.

Divine Appointment

Come with me and meet the Samaritan woman at the well.

1. Please read **John 4:1-26** and answer the following questions.

a. Record your observations about this encounter. There are many Biblical lessons we could extract from this story, but for our purposes here we will focus on the woman.

b. Do you think Jesus knew He was going to meet the woman at the well? Why?

c. Why do you think the woman came to draw her water from the well at the sixth hour? (noon, the hottest time of day; most other women would come early in the morning or in the cool of the evening)

d. The woman in this story was a Samaritan. Jesus was Jewish. Jews in that day did not associate with Samaritans since they were a mixed race and seen as unclean sinners. Most Jews of the day would take the long way around just to avoid traveling through the region of Samaria. Yet Jesus, the perfect, sinless Savior, took the direct route that all others avoided on His journey just to meet this special woman. Does the woman seem surprised that Jesus would speak to her? What do you think was going through her mind?

e. How does Jesus describe the water that He has to offer her? See verses **4:10, 13-14**.

f. Describe the woman's love life.

g. Does she seem to be trying to fill a void in her life? If so, how?

    h.   What is her response when Jesus brings up her past and present living situations?

Jesus begins the conversation by asking her for a drink of water. She is surprised that Jesus would even speak to her since she is a Samaritan, a woman, and an outcast even among her own people. But the love of Jesus crosses all boundaries. Her weaknesses, her sins, and her past could not keep Him from pursuing her.

Jesus knew this woman's pain; He knew every detail of her life. It was all laid bare before Him. Through their conversation we learn that the woman, for whatever reason, had been married five times and was currently living with her boyfriend. She may have been trying to fill the void in her heart with these various relationships, but none would ever fully meet her needs or make her feel complete. Jesus came to offer her the only thing that would fully satisfy the thirst and longing of her heart—He offered Himself, the Living Water. She could finally stop searching for something, or someone else to fill her up.

We notice that when Jesus brought up her situation, she quickly tried to change the subject. Like the woman, we don't like to look at our sins, or acknowledge our weaknesses. It seems so much easier to keep them hidden and try to forget them. We keep them stuffed down inside, dreading the shame we will feel if they are exposed. Jesus has a better plan though. He wants to bring everything into the light so it can be dealt with out in the open.

Jesus didn't bring up her past to shame her, He exposed it so He could heal her. Jesus had her come face-to-face with the reality of her life so it could be dealt with, so that she could be free to move forward with Him, able to receive His Living water which would bubble up and continually refresh her soul.

    i.   How was her life transformed after her encounter with Jesus? See verses **4:27-29**.

    j.   Read verses **4:39-42**. How were the lives of others impacted as a result of her encounter with Jesus?

This woman began a new life as she encountered Jesus that day. Her shame was gone. The same people she had previously avoided, she now ran to so she could share the hope and message of Jesus' redemption. She wanted everyone to meet the Messiah. The love, acceptance, hope, joy and life-transforming power of Jesus radically changed her. She gained a confidence she never had before. She was so excited about Jesus that she wanted everyone else to know Him. Her testimony had an amazing impact on everyone who heard it.

Jesus told us to be prepared to give an answer for the hope we have in Him. Our testimonies have a great impact. As others see the miraculous change in us, they want to know Jesus too. I am positive that many people will be greatly encouraged as you share how God has transformed your life. As we come to know the love that God has for us, our confidence grows abundantly, equipping us to proudly testify to His power and love which is available to all.

Personal Reflection

Geography and roadways didn't make Jesus take this avoidable route. Love did. He had a divine appointment with a needy soul, a hurting woman who needed His love, healing and redemption. Like the woman at the well, Jesus came purposefully for you and me. He knows every single detail about us and loves us deeply in spite of it. Our past and present don't keep Him away; He came to give us a future.

2. Please put yourself in the place of the woman in the story. Picture yourself having this encounter with Jesus and answer the following questions.

    a. How does it feel to know that Jesus went out of His way to meet you where you were/are?

    b. God's love is not earned; it is not merit based. **God's love is unconditional**; it is the one certainty you can count on in life. Do you realize that Jesus knows every detail of your life and loves you anyway? What emotion comes to mind as you discover this truth: surprise, shame, fear, relief, joy, hope, peace, gratitude, etc.?

    c. What are some ways that you try to fill the void in your heart? Or ways that people in general try to fill their void?

d. How has your life been transformed by your encounter with Jesus? If you have not yet encountered Jesus, would you like to know Him and His unconditional love?

Jesus knows how your heart aches and longs to be loved. He knows all the ways you have tried to fill your heart and have still been left wanting. He knows that the depths of your heart and soul can only be satisfied with the heights of His love.

Psalm 42:1, "As the deer pants for streams of water, so my soul pants for you, my God."

We often overlook that our souls are thirsting, so we try to fill ourselves with temporary fixes. As the old country song says, we are "Lookin' for love in all the wrong places." We look to different relationships and roles to fill us up; we look to them for our identity, security, and sense of worth. We sometimes look to pills, drugs, or alcohol as an escape, but that only leads to more loneliness and isolation. Or sometimes we think we can earn love and acceptance through hard work and being a good girl.

You know, sadly, it is possible to be a Christian and still be looking for love, acceptance, and completion apart from Christ; we know that our salvation comes from Jesus, but we haven't grasped the love He has for us. Love is the whole reason He came to bring us salvation in the first place.

We must surrender our hearts to Him, to be filled with His love. No one else can meet all our needs, and no one else was ever meant to. Every person on this planet comes with their own personal baggage; we're all flawed and imperfect people. Only Jesus, God in the flesh, is perfect, and only He can fill us perfectly. It's time to believe Jesus for our salvation, and believe Him for all the rest… He's big enough to fill our emptiness completely. Like the woman at the well, all our needs are met in Him alone. He loves us unconditionally; He knows how we are made and what we need. We are made to first be filled with God's love, and then we can enjoy other relationships for what they have to offer, taking the pressure off them to be our "everything." Jesus is our "everything." All other relationships are icing on the cake.

Jesus came to fill us with His love so that we no longer need to search to be filled by anything or anyone else ever again. He is The Living Water. Just as our bodies thirst for water, so our souls thirst for God.

Psalm 63:1-8, "You, God, are my God, earnestly I seek you; I thirst for you, my whole being longs for you, in a dry and parched land where there is no water. 2 I have seen you in the sanctuary and beheld your power and your glory. 3 Because your love is better than life, my lips will glorify you. 4 I will praise you as long as I live, and in your name I will lift up my hands. 5 I will be fully satisfied as with the richest of foods; with singing lips my mouth will praise you. 6 On my bed I remember you; I think of you through the watches of the night. 7 Because you are my help, I sing in the shadow of your wings 8 I cling to you; your right hand upholds me."

3. In **Psalm 63:1-8**, what imagery does the psalmist use to describe our desire for God?

4. Imagine being thirsty/hungry—how do you feel when your appetite is yearning for something specific to fill you? How do you feel when that craving is met?

5. Write your personal reflections on **Psalm 63:1-8** here:

6. If you are not yet thirsting for Jesus, take time now to pray and ask the Lord to make you thirst for Him. He fully satisfies!

God's Gift of Love

I have received some wonderful gifts in my lifetime. Some big, some small, some store-bought, some handmade, some sentimental, some practical. What really makes a gift special is the thought behind it, knowing that someone was specifically thinking of you.

One Christmas years ago, when I was still a teenager, a loved one gave me a gift that I still have. It is a small, clear plastic toolbox with a green handle and a green latch which snaps closed, keeping the contents safe within. It holds screwdrivers of every size, even the teeny-tiny ones for tightening eyeglasses, it has a hammer, a measuring tape, a level, staples, thumb tacks, and a stapler. It seems every tool imaginable is tucked neatly inside this small toolbox. To this day I am prepared for whatever job that comes my way. Who would have guessed that all these years later, I would still be using this gift, a gift my loved one thought would come in handy?

7. Is there a special gift someone once gave to you that comes to mind? Describe.

8. Do you know someone who seems to have a great ability to give good gifts? If so, who?

There is a Gift that is perfect in every way, and it's given by the best gift giver of all, God Himself!

As believers, we get to reflect on the love that God has towards us every day. But each year as Christmas approaches, we see celebrations of His love everywhere. The season inspires us to give gifts to show our love to others. But God was the first One to ever give a Christmas gift. (You can find the story of the first Christmas Gift in Luke 2—my favorite chapter in the Bible)

2 Corinthians 9:15, "Thanks be to God for his indescribable gift!"

9. Please read **John 3:16** and answer the following questions.

   a. What Gift did God give?

   b. What was the motivation for God's Gift (why did He give it)?

Hebrews 12:2, "For the joy set before him he endured the cross, scorning its shame, and sat down at the right hand of the throne of God."

10. According to **Hebrews 12:2,** what/who do think the "joy" represents?

The motivation for God's Gift was love! God put a lot of thought into the Gift He gave for you. Driven by love, God came to save the whole world. His love is also personal and intimate, He came to save *you*. God desires to have a relationship with you so much that He gave His Son, Jesus Christ to die in your place on the cross. God gave up *everything*, just to have *you* for Himself. Jesus' mission was to redeem and restore *you*. YOU are the joy set before Jesus while He went to the cross. *You* were on His mind! The thought of eternity with *YOU* brings Jesus great joy, and that is what helped Him endure the agony of the cross.

11. What emotions and thoughts come to mind as you reflect on the *priceless Gift* God has given to you, and for you?

12. Look up the following Scriptures and record the blessings that accompany God's Gift.

- **Romans 6:23**

- **Luke 11:13**

- **Ephesians 1:17-18**

- **Romans 11:29**

God offers us the priceless Gift of His Son Jesus; because He loves us immensely and wants to spend all of eternity with us. Like the giver of my little toolbox, He also wants us to have the tools for whatever comes our way in life here on earth. Wrapped up in Jesus, we have everything we will ever need: salvation through His death on the cross, the promise of eternal life with our Heavenly Father through His resurrection, His Holy Spirit indwelling in us—to accompany and guide us through each and every day; we also have His joy and peace to flood our hearts with His heavenly perspective, and His love and hope to carry us onward till we see Him face-to-face.

Psalm 36:5, "Your love, LORD, reaches to the heavens, your faithfulness to the skies."

God's Love Letter

In this age of texting and emails, I love getting the surprise of opening the mailbox to find an old-fashioned, handwritten card or letter, and obviously I am not the only one. Greeting cards remain a very popular way of letting others know that they are in our thoughts; they carry words of encouragement, of celebration and congratulations, of sympathy and condolences. Greeting cards are written conveyances of our love to others. Some people store away and save the cards they receive—regarding them as treasures to keep in a box for future times, to reread and reflect upon. Another written expression of love can be shared in a letter or simple note. When I was younger, my boyfriend—now husband—would deliver love letters and pictures to me that he had written and drawn while he was supposed to be paying attention to his college lectures. Even today, he will occasionally leave me a note, often with a silly cartoon drawing on it. These continue to be little reminders of his love for me.

God has written a letter declaring His love for us. It is called the Bible. The pages of the Bible, from Genesis through Revelation, are filled with the story of God's love, and the great lengths He continually goes to just to capture our hearts. The promises that accompany His unending love are also found within the covers of this Holy Book. God's love letter has endured through the centuries and is meant to be read daily as a reminder of His love for us.

I absolutely love Scripture. It is my foundation for Truth in this crazy world. Any time I wrestle with doubts or discouragements, or I forget who I am in Christ Jesus and all the blessings that come along with my relationship with Him, I go back to Scripture to remind myself of the truth. The Bible helps keep my life on track. I encourage you to read His love letter often for yourself.

13. Please look up the following verses and note some of the descriptions of God's love found in Scripture (God's love letter).

- **Psalm 5:7**

- **Psalm 5:12**

- **Psalm 94:18**

- **Psalm 23:6**

- **Deuteronomy 31:6-8**

Know God, Know Love

I grew up knowing that God loved me, and I received Jesus as my Savior when I was 12. But I was 30 years old on the day I felt His love truly wash over me. I was at church alone that morning, standing up in the balcony area. There was a guy on stage, he was playing the piano and singing a song all about God's love for us. As I stood there singing along, I felt the Holy Spirit envelop me, and a flood of God's love wash over me. I began silently sobbing, tears flowing down my cheeks as I bowed my head. I tried to keep my body from shaking since I was crying so hard. God's love utterly pierced my heart that morning. The love of God has changed my life like nothing else possibly could.

There is a love song that my Grandma taught me as a child— a love song that brings me joy and comfort— and I am certain many of you may know it too. It is a simple yet profound song, and the verse is one that should play constantly through our minds. **"Jesus loves me this I know, for the Bible tells me so."** If the Bible says it, it must be true.

Romans 8:39, "Neither height nor depth, nor anything else in all creation, will be able to separate us from the love of God that is in Christ Jesus our Lord."

Nothing can ever separate you from God's love! Nothing, not ever!

14. Have you ever experienced such devoted love before? How does this *eternal commitment* of love make you feel?

Ephesians 3:17-19, "I pray that you, being rooted and established in love, ¹⁸ may have power, together with all the Lord's holy people, to grasp how wide and long and high and deep is the love of Christ, ¹⁹ and to know this love that surpasses knowledge—that you may be filled to the measure of all the fullness of God."

While Bible study is an essential part of our Christian walk, some people approach it with the purpose of gaining and retaining intellectual knowledge of Biblical details rather than seeking to know God and His love more personally. A life is transformed when God's love touches a heart, not when a mind is filled with mere knowledge *about* Him. His love surpasses all human understanding and is beyond anything we have previously known on earth. Knowledge of His love is made possible through revelation from His Spirit directly to our hearts and minds.

I pray this prayer for my loved ones and for myself because there is nothing more important than for us to comprehend the enormous love that God has for us.

15. Take a moment and pray the **Ephesians 3:17-19** prayer for yourself, asking God to help you grasp His amazing love for you.

1 John 4:8, 19, "Whoever does not love does not know God, because God is love...We love because he first loved us."

16. According to **1 John 4:8, 19**, where does love come from? What is the very nature of God?

1 Corinthians 13:4-8, "Love is patient, love is kind. It does not envy, it does not boast, it is not proud. ⁵ It does not dishonor others, it is not self-seeking, it is not easily angered, it keeps no record of wrongs. ⁶ Love does not delight in evil but rejoices with the truth. ⁷ It always protects, always trusts, always hopes, always perseveres. ⁸ Love never fails."

17. Slowly re-read **1 Corinthians 13:4-8** and answer the following questions.

    a. According to the Scriptures, what does true love look like?

    b. Which description of love stands out to you the most?

    c. For which attribute of love is your heart most yearning?

    d. Are you confident that God can love you like this? Ask Him to help you trust His love.

Others may have hurt us in the past, or even be hurting us presently. We may have entrusted our heart to the care of someone who was not completely trustworthy. We may have been betrayed or mistreated. Others may have failed to love us as we need, desire, and deserve. So often the love we experience is very different than the love the Bible describes. Scripture tells us "True love never fails." That's a high standard to reach! God is the only one who can love so perfectly. We are to try—with the help of the Holy Spirit to love like this— but only God can truly love so perfectly. *His* love NEVER fails; it doesn't give up on us, it never hurts, it doesn't depend on our performance or our behavior. His love is unconditional. He never withholds His love from us. If we don't feel His love, it's because we are not paying attention, or because we have withdrawn from Him. His love never fails!

1 Chronicles 16:34, "Give thanks to the LORD, for he is good! His love endures forever."

We don't earn His love by our behavior, but His precious love inspires us to live a life that pleases Him.

Our Response to His love

18. Please read the following verses and record the response we are to have to God's love.

- **John 14:15-24**

- **Matthew 22:36-40**

- **1 John 2:5-6**

- **Deuteronomy 13:3-4**

- **Deuteronomy 30:6**

- **Deuteronomy 30:20**

- **1 Kings 8:23**

- **1 John 4:7-12**

One last example I would like to share with you regarding the confidence that comes from God's love is found throughout the Gospel of John. Whenever John—the author—relays a story, he includes the names of all who are involved, but when he should include his own name, he doesn't call himself John, but rather "the disciple whom Jesus loved." That's some pretty serious confidence in his Savior's love! John went on to write the letters of 1, 2, and 3 John, the majority of which are devoted to the topic of God's love. Near the end of his life, he also scribed the book of Revelation, which speaks of Jesus returning to earth to reunite with all His beloved. John had confidence, hope, courage, and joy because he was filled with the love of God.

My hope is that through the pages of Scripture, you have begun to view yourself as "the woman whom Jesus loves," and that you confidently believe His love is unconditional, irrevocable, endless, and sincere.

I pray that as you are filled with the love of God and gain confidence as His child, secure in His love, that you—like the woman at the well—will now go out and courageously love others in the name of Jesus, letting them know of His amazing love for them.

The love of God propels us forward to live in confidence; the love of God compels us to reach out beyond ourselves.

The Simple Truth: God loves you!

A Simple Prayer: Dear Lord, thank you for loving me with Your perfect, unconditional love. Please fill my heart with Your life-giving, thirst-quenching love so I stop searching for completeness apart from You. Help me to gain confidence in the security of Your loving arms. Amen.

"I pray that you, being rooted and established in love, may have power, together with all the Lord's holy people, to grasp how wide and long and high and deep is the love of Christ, and to know this love that surpasses knowledge—that you may be filled to the measure of all the fullness of God."

Ephesians 3:17-19

Write out your own prayer in response to the immeasurable love that God has for you:

CHAPTER TWO

You are Forgiven and New

Throughout this chapter, the most important thing for you to remember is that, *"There is now no condemnation for those who are in Christ Jesus." Romans 8:1*

Our need for a Savior

Since the fall of Adam and Eve way back in the Garden of Eden (Genesis 3), every human has been under the curse of sin. Sin is any rebellion against God— any thought or action contrary to the knowledge, nature, and authority of God. Some of you know too well the reality of your sins; you carry around the shame, regret, and burden like a heavy weight on your soul—for the record, God wants to take that burden from you. Others of you might be thinking, "I'm okay with God because I'm a pretty good person, I don't do bad things, and I try to be nice to others." But if you're truly honest with yourself, you'll admit your need for a Savior. Jesus says our sins begin in our hearts and minds and are then exhibited through our actions and words. Even if our actions aren't so bad, what's going on behind the scenes, inside our heads can be ugly.

If you took just a snapshot of your life—pick one day, any day you like—would you feel comfortable having every thought exposed? Would you still feel righteous in your own effort? If I'm honest with myself, I definitely wouldn't. I need help, I need a Savior! Some mornings before my feet even hit the floor, I need help.

We know ourselves better than anyone—anyone, that is except our Heavenly Father. He knows us inside and out: all our weaknesses, our flaws and faults, all the things we regret and would rather forget. He knows things about us that we don't even recognize about ourselves. He knows it all and loves us in spite of it. God accepts us just as we are but loves us so much that He refuses to leave us that way. He has a much better life in store for us!

What appears hopeless to us has great possibility with God. He can and does forgive every sin imaginable once we accept Jesus Christ as our Lord and Savior—He wipes the slate clean, giving us a new identity as His child. Now, *that* is something to celebrate!

1. Please read **Romans 3:22-26** and answer the following questions.

   Romans 3:22-26, "This righteousness is given through faith in Jesus Christ to all who believe. There is no difference between Jew and Gentile, ²³ for all have sinned and fall short of the glory of God, ²⁴ and all are justified freely by his grace through the redemption that came by Christ Jesus. ²⁵ God presented Christ as a sacrifice of atonement, through the shedding of his blood—to be received by faith. He did this to demonstrate his righteousness, because in his forbearance he had left the sins committed beforehand unpunished— ²⁶ he did it to demonstrate his righteousness at the present time, so as to be just and the one who justifies those who have faith in Jesus."

   a. Who has sinned and fallen short of the glory of God?

   b. How is righteousness—God's judicial approval, to be deemed right by the LORD—obtained?

   c. Who is justified (judged, regarded, or treated as righteous and worthy of salvation) and freely forgiven? How?

   d. What is God's part in our salvation?

   e. What is our part in our salvation?

God's Word says, "All have sinned and fall short of the glory of God." I hope you noticed that you are not alone in your shortcomings! On our own, none of us reach God's glorious and holy standard. We are all in need of a Savior— you and me and everyone! Scripture says it doesn't matter what our backgrounds are, we all need Jesus. God saw the sin that holds the whole world in bondage and provided The Way to set us free from its clutches. Because of His great love for us and by His amazing grace, He sent His Son to die on the cross, to take the punishment that our sin deserves. God has redeemed us (delivered us, and by the blood of Jesus has purchased us back from the shackles of sin). His sacrifice—giving His life for ours—makes us right with God. We are *not* made right by our own effort or goodness but by placing our *faith* in the *grace* that God has *freely* given. Jesus paid the price once and for all. As He hung on the cross, "Jesus said, 'It is finished.' With that, he bowed his head and gave up his spirit." John 19:30

In Jesus your forgiveness is a done deal!

Confidently Confess

Even though we know our salvation is secure, sometimes we may still encounter moments of doubt, and feel that we're beyond all help or hope, and even be ready to give up on ourselves, but God never gives up on us. He has a plan to restore us, refresh us, and bring new life to us. He is the One who empowers us to overcome our sins and bravely face the future. God redeems all our life experiences—the good, the bad, the ugly. God looks at our messy lives and sees the beautiful potential in them. There is absolutely nothing in our lives that God cannot redeem us from or transform into something good. With God, nothing is ever wasted. He takes the old and makes it new.

According to Webster's dictionary the definition of Redeem is:
1. To buy back: REPURCHASE; to get or win back
2. To free from what distresses or harms: as to free from captivity by payment of ransom; to extricate from or help to overcome something detrimental or harmful
3. To release from blame or debt: CLEAR; to free from the consequences of sin
4. To change for the better: REFORM, REPAIR, RESTORE

This is exactly what God does with us!

We need only be willing to turn everything over to Him and allow Him to work His mighty miracles in our lives.

　　2. The beautiful process of redemption begins with our surrendering it all to God. Confession is a vital part of our surrender. Please look up the following verses and write down what you learn about the power of confession.

- **Romans 10:9-10**

- **1 John 1:9**

- **Psalm 32:5**

3. Now let's look at what happens when we try to keep our sin hidden.

    - **Psalm 32:3-4**

    - **Psalm 38:18**

    - **Proverbs 28:13**

When we keep our sins buried deep within us, locked inside as a secret, we are held captive with shame, and with fear that we'll be found out. There is no joy in living like this, but great joy and freedom are found as we just lay it all out before the Lord.

4. Read the following verse and note the blessing that comes from sharing our burdens with others.

    - **James 5:16**

We are not meant to be on this journey alone. When we open up to others—like our fellow sisters-in-Christ— and allow them to pray with us and support us in releasing our sin, we are blessed with relief, peace, and comfort as they help us carry our burden to the Lord.

Confession brings endless blessings—the confession of our need for Jesus brings salvation, and the confession of our sin brings forgiveness and healing. Take a few moments to reflect on your own life. Pray and confess your need for a Savior and your belief in Jesus Christ. Then ask God to bring any sin—thought, word or action— that you need to repent of to your mind and ask Him for forgiveness. Two more things I encourage you to pray for: God's help and strength to leave the sin behind, and also His help in forgiving yourself—this is vitally important in the healing process.

Hebrews 4:14-16, "Therefore, since we have a great high priest who has ascended into heaven, Jesus the Son of God, let us hold firmly to the faith we profess. ¹⁵ For we do not have a high priest who is unable to empathize with our weaknesses, but we have one who has been tempted in every way, just as we are—yet he did not sin. ¹⁶ Let us then approach God's throne of grace with confidence, so that we may receive mercy and find grace to help us in our time of need."

No matter what you've done, you can confidently—without fear—approach the throne of God. He is more than willing to forgive any and all of your sins and help you in any way you need. Just ask Him.

5. Please read the following verses and let these Psalms be the prayers of your own heart.

- **Psalm 25:7**

- **Psalm 40:11**

- **Psalm 119:132**

God is faithful to answer each and every one of these prayers. He turns to us, and showers us in His mercy, love, and faithfulness. He forgives and forgets our sins—the ones we made when we were young, or ignorant, or just outright rebellious. He doesn't hold them against us or throw them back in our face. Ever. He is good.

Psalm 103:1-12. "Praise the LORD, my soul; all my inmost being, praise his holy name. ² Praise the LORD, my soul, and forget not all his benefits— ³ who forgives all your sins and heals all your diseases, ⁴ who redeems your life from the pit and crowns you with love and compassion, ⁵ who satisfies your desires with good things so that your youth is renewed like the eagle's. ⁶ The LORD works righteousness and justice for all the oppressed. ⁷ He made known his ways to Moses, his deeds to the people of Israel: ⁸ The LORD is compassionate and gracious, slow to anger, abounding in love. ⁹ He will not always accuse, nor will he harbor his anger forever; ¹⁰ he does not treat us as our sins deserve or repay us according to our iniquities. ¹¹ For as high as the heavens are above the earth, so great is his love for those who fear him; ¹² as far as the east is from the west, so far has he removed our transgressions from us."

6. According to **Psalm 103:1-12**, list all the benefits of turning your life over to the LORD.

On top of the countless benefits and blessings that God bestows on you, I hope you notice just how far God removes the guilt of your sins from you: "As far as the east is from the west." Try to imagine just how far this is—your sins are completely removed from you.

No Condemnation

Let's look at a woman who experienced the grace and forgiveness of Jesus first-hand.

7. Please read **John 8:1-11** and answer the following questions.

a. What accusations are being hurled against the woman?

b. What does the crowd want done to her because of her sin?

c. How does Jesus respond to those in the crowd?

d. What are Jesus' words to the woman?

e. After Jesus graciously forgives the woman, what command does He give her?

f. Do you ever feel condemned or accused by others? If so, how?

g. How do you feel knowing that this is not how Jesus treats you?

Again, we could dissect this story and take away many Biblical lessons, but for the purpose of our study—Forgiven and New—we will focus on the woman at the center of it all. This woman encountered Jesus on what was probably one of the worst, most shameful days of her life. You may even say this was her version of hitting rock bottom, and there was no other place to look or to turn for help, but into her Savior's eyes. Her sin had been exposed before everyone, including Jesus. Yet Jesus looked on her with grace and mercy, not harshness, shame, or condemnation. Though others condemned and wanted to stone her, He saw her aching heart and He defended her. He showed her forgiveness and offered her a new beginning. After the woman encountered Jesus, her life was forever changed with the knowledge that He was her personal defender. Experiencing His forgiveness would have most likely filled her with a new confidence, one that would help her move forward, leaving the past behind her.

"'Then neither do I condemn you,' Jesus declared. 'Go now and leave your life of sin.'"

Our new life in Christ demands that we too leave our old lives of sin.

2 Timothy 2:19, "'The Lord knows those who are his,' and, 'Everyone who confesses the name of the Lord must turn away from wickedness.'"

As a child of God, we must leave our sins behind. Sin is no longer our option.

You are a New Creation

Ephesians 4:22-24, "You were taught, with regard to your former way of life, to put off your old self, which is being corrupted by its deceitful desires; 23 to be made new in the attitude of your minds; 24 and to put on the new self, created to be like God in true righteousness and holiness."

Based on the description in Scripture, I picture my *old* sinful self like a shabby overcoat that's worn out in the seams, with holes in the elbows, stains down the front, and terribly ugly, and I am so grateful that God has allowed me to take it off and trade it in for a new, clean, stain-free, radiant, outer garment of His righteousness.

Revelation 19:8, "'Fine linen, bright and clean, was given her to wear.' (Fine linen stands for the righteous acts of God's holy people.)"

8. Do you believe God when He says you are forgiven?

9. Do you still see yourself in your old shabby overcoat? Or do you see yourself as you truly are, clothed in a bright clean garment of righteousness? Explain.

10. Do thoughts of regret and shame ever invade your mind? Have you learned to turn them over to God? Explain.

11. How easily do you forgive yourself for past or recent sins? Remember how important this step is in moving you forward.

If you have put your faith in the sacrifice of Jesus, then this is exactly how God sees you: new, clean and pure, blameless and sinless! And if this is how God sees you, then don't you think it's about time you see yourself this way too?

Many of our poor decisions in life are rooted in insecurities. Just think of all the shame and regret that can be avoided going forward if we make choices based on the confidence we have as a child of God. Although we can't go back and change our past, we *can* stop beating ourselves up over it, accept God's forgiveness, and move forward in confidence! If God says we are forgiven, then it has to be true. We must believe Him!

Even if we believe God, sometimes thoughts of our past sins and mistakes—that have long been forgiven by God—unexpectedly pop into our minds. It's what we do with these thoughts that matters—we can let them run wild in our heads, bringing shame and condemnation; we can let them steal the joy and hope of the forgiveness and freedom we have found in Jesus, or we can turn our thoughts over to God and let Him fill us with the reassuring, reaffirming Truth that we are indeed already forgiven.

Philippians 4:8, "Finally, brothers and sisters, whatever is true, whatever is noble, whatever is right, whatever is pure, whatever is lovely, whatever is admirable—if anything is excellent or praiseworthy—think about such things."

The truth is we are God's new creation and we've been washed clean.

2 Corinthians 5:17, "Therefore, if anyone is in Christ, the new creation has come: The old has gone, the new is here!"

That's you! The old you has gone, the new you is here to stay!

Since we've been washed clean, we now want to stay that way, and fortunately Scripture gives us a game-plan for staying clean.

Psalm 119:80, "May I wholeheartedly follow your decrees, that I may not be put to shame."

Reading our Bible and living by what it says (not by what our feelings say, what our friends or families say, or what Satan our enemy says) is our sure-fire way to keep from sinning, and this will help us to avoid future regret.

Our New Life has a New Focus

We are new, but Jesus must remain our focus!

12. Please read **Hebrews 12:1-2** and make a note of the helpful encouragements on how to keep yourself sin-free.

    a. How are we to run? What does this mean to you?

    b. Where is our focus to be?

Here Scripture has described life as a race, a race that every person is entered into upon birth. Once our race begins, **we have a choice in how we will run it**—unintentionally (meandering aimlessly), carelessly (bumping into everything), distractedly (looking everywhere but ahead), or with deliberate focus, purpose, and goals.

How *well* we run our race depends greatly on our choices and our focus.

Placing our faith in Jesus for our salvation, following Him daily, and leaving our lives of sin behind are choices we deliberately make during our race. Once we decide to follow Jesus we are saved from our sins and from the threat of death. We must, however, intentionally choose to prevent sin from hindering and entangling us daily. How do we do this? Not on our own, that's for sure. Only by running the race with Jesus, locking our eyes steadfastly on Him, letting Him lead us onward to victory. He is the pioneer, blazing the trail before us.

When I read this verse I get a picture of my race and Jesus is filling all the roles- Jesus is my trainer, getting me prepared and keeping me well-conditioned physically, spiritually and mentally; He is on the sidelines cheering me on, saying, "Keep going, you can do it!"; He is my partner, running side-by-side with me every step of the way; He is my coach, calling me on toward Himself, the finish line and victory.

2 Timothy 4:7-8, "I have fought the good fight, I have finished the race, I have kept the faith. ⁸ Now there is in store for me the crown of righteousness, which the Lord, the righteous Judge, will award to me on that day—and not only to me, but also to all who have longed for his appearing."

I don't know about you, but at the end of my life I'd love to repeat these confident words of Paul's as my very own.

His Joy, Our Joy

Jesus had intentional focus as He lived out His purpose here on earth. His focus was Joy. Joy was waiting at the finish line of His life.

Hebrews 12:2, "For *the joy* set before him he endured the cross, scorning its shame, and sat down at the right hand of the throne of God."

We looked at this verse briefly in chapter one, but let's dig a little deeper and savor its meaning. What is this joy that Jesus was so focused on? *You* are the joy; *I* am the joy that was set before Jesus. The thought of our salvation and a restored relationship with us were on Jesus' mind as He hung on the cross; our forgiveness was His goal, and our redemption was His purpose. Jesus endured the agony of the cross for *the joy* of *us* being with Him for all eternity. Jesus' sacrifice paid to ransom us from our sins, and He considered it a joy to give up His life for our sake. While on the cross, Jesus proclaimed the words, "It is finished" (John 19:30). With His purpose and joy complete, Jesus is now exalted and seated at the right hand of God the Father in the heavenly realms until the time He returns for us.

Now *the joy* set before *me*, and *the joy* set before *you* is to die to self and live for Jesus Christ our Savior, and for His Gospel message. We no longer live for ourselves; we instead live for Him. *Our joy* is to know Him, to obey Him, to glorify Him, to love Him and to praise Him with everything we have! We are to continue in the same joy that Jesus had on the cross at Calvary and take up our own cross daily. Someday we will see Him face-to-face, and we too will be exalted in the Kingdom of Heaven, but until that day, we will seek to follow and honor Him here on earth. This joy should be our focus.

13. Do you see living for Jesus as a "joy"? What does it mean to you personally to experience joy on a daily basis while living for Jesus?

14. What are some practical ways we can all take up our cross daily? How do you plan on implementing these in your own life? What can you personally surrender to Him? In what ways can you start living more for Him?

Fresh Mercies, Every Day

Even though we are counted righteous and washed clean of the stain of our sins, we may occasionally and momentarily fall into our old sins and our old habits while on this journey. A word may slip out, we might do something we know we shouldn't have. We may let go of Jesus' hand, get distracted and venture off on our own in the wrong direction for a second. Fortunately, we can never mess up badly enough that God's grace and mercy cannot redeem and forgive us. Neither will our sins ever separate us from His love.

Ephesians 2:8-9, "For it is by grace you have been saved, through faith—and this is not from yourselves, it is the gift of God— ⁹ not by works, so that no one can boast."

Let me re-emphasize this: we are saved by placing our faith in Jesus Christ, by the grace of God alone. We don't earn His grace by anything good that we do, and *we can't lose His grace by anything bad we do.*

In the security of God's grace, we find a reason for confidence.

The confidence we speak of throughout this study is not a worldly, self-reliant confidence, but a holy God-reliant one. I thought I would share the Biblical meaning of the word "confidence," which I found on the website Biblestudytools.com.

Confidence: *certainty and assurance of one's relationship with God, a sense of boldness that is dependent on a realization of one's acceptance by God, and a conviction that one's destiny is secure in God.*

15. Please read the following verses and make note of the security found in God's mercy.

    - **Lamentations 3:22-23**

    - **John 10:28-30**

    - **Ephesians 4:30**

Daily mercies. No fear of losing our salvation. We are forever sealed with God's Spirit. All reasons for confidence.

God the Father offers and gives us a fresh life through Jesus Christ not just when we accept Him as Savior, but also daily as we come before Him and confess and repent of our sins. That means we get a do-over every day.

I love to receive gifts sets; they are always packaged so perfectly pretty. One Christmas my dear sister gave me one of these delightful gift sets, it included body wash and lotion. When I opened the bottle, it smelled soft, sweet, and fresh, and the name on the label actually read, "Fresh Life." I love the symbolism of the name. Who doesn't want a fresh life, a fresh start? When I first received it, momentarily thought, "Wouldn't it be great if I could get a fresh life just by lathering this body wash all over myself every day?" Then I quickly remembered I have something better. I already have the daily cleansing, and a fresh life from God continually pouring over me by the grace of Jesus.

Even though I am eternally washed clean, there are days, or moments that I could use a fresh start—a do-over—to take back my words, take my back actions; times I'd like to take an eraser and remove whatever it is that I did completely from history. I'm so grateful this is more than wishful thinking.

Example of a Do-Over

Let's look at a Biblical example of a major do-over.

16. If there was ever anyone who wanted to take back his words, anyone who desperately wanted a do-over, it was Peter. Please read his story in the following three passages of Scripture and record your thoughts on the situation. What does Jesus know and say to Peter? How does Peter respond? How does Peter feel? Describe the situation. Describe the grace and mercy of Jesus.

The first part of the story takes place before Jesus' arrest.

- **Matthew 26:34-35**

The next excerpt occurs after Jesus' arrest.

- **Matthew 26:69-75**

The third portion of Peter's story takes place after the death, burial, and resurrection of Jesus. The scene takes place early in the morning on the shore of Lake Tiberias, as Peter and the other disciples, weary and tired, are just coming in from a long night of fishing, only to find Jesus waiting for them. This was the third time He had appeared to them since His resurrection. The following conversation takes place as the disciples enjoy a meal with their Risen Savior.

- **John 21:15-19**

In the progression of the story, we notice that Jesus foreknew Peter was going to give into temptation and fail, even to the point of denying that he knew Jesus. Jesus predicted exactly how many times Peter would deny Him and the precise time frame within which he would do it: three times, before the rooster crowed. And early the next morning as the rooster did crow, Peter, overcome with shame and regret, wept as the words of Jesus, and his very own words of denial hauntingly played through his mind. Peter needed a serious do-over and Jesus, His Lord and Savior was faithful to give it. This early morning scene when the resurrected Jesus met His disciples on the shore, it was with the purpose of restoring Peter. In His mercy, Jesus gave Peter the opportunity for redemption. Jesus didn't bring up Peter's past and throw it in his face, but instead met Peter in his place of repentance and offered him a chance for full and complete restoration. Jesus took Peter's words of denial and redeemed them with words of acceptance—three times Peter had denied his Lord, and three times Jesus gave the opportunity for Peter to proclaim his love and commitment to his Savior and Friend. Jesus is our great Redeemer. He takes our hopeless weaknesses, our big mistakes, and our deliberate sins, and He turns them into life lessons, while offering us each a fresh start.

We are daughters of the King. Our salvation is secure, our forgiveness is complete. Yet, as we live here on earth awaiting the day we reside in the Heavenly Kingdom, we will occasionally exhibit un-heavenly behavior. I find wonderful encouragement in knowing even great heroes of the faith like Peter and Paul struggled daily with weakness. Paul wrote about his struggle in **Romans 7:15-20: "I do not understand what I do. For what I want to do I do not do, but what I hate I do."** I thank God for His patient grace and transforming power in me.

17. How does Peter's story offer us hope and encouragement to persevere in our faith—to not give up, even when we mess up, but to continually move forward?

18. Describe a time when Jesus offered you a do-over.

Cleaned Up and Ready for Service

I want to share with you one last story of an individual who experienced God's forgiveness, and the powerful way it impacted their life.

19. Please read **Isaiah 6:1-8** and answer the following questions.

a. Describe the scene that Isaiah is witnessing. How does Isaiah feel in the presence of such holiness?

b. What is Isaiah's response when his guilt is taken away, and his sin is atoned for?

c. What is your response to the forgiveness of your sin?

Like Isaiah, we have encountered our Holy God, we stand awed by His glory and amazed at His grace. Having been cleansed of our sin, with new confidence we can also say "Here I am! Send me!"

Forgiven and Confident

We know what we were, and we know what we are now, and out of gratitude we now live for Him, not our own glory, but for His.

Each one of us who has been redeemed by God becomes a poster child of His goodness, love, and power through Jesus Christ. As His children, we each have sin that has been forgiven, we each have a life that's been transformed, and we each have a story to tell, a story that brings glory to God, our Heavenly Father.

Psalm 107:1-2, "Give thanks to the LORD, for he is good; his love endures forever. ² Let the redeemed of the LORD tell their story— those he redeemed from the hand of the foe."

The Simple Truth: You are forgiven and new!

A Simple Prayer: Dear Merciful Father, thank you for forgiving and rescuing me from my sin. Help me to stop beating myself up over the past, and gain confidence in the fact that I am a new creation in Christ Jesus. Help me to walk forward with You in freedom. Amen.

"If we confess our sins, he is faithful and just and will forgive us our sins and purify us from all unrighteousness." 1 John 1:9

Take a moment to reflect on God's lavish grace and write out a prayer of gratitude in response:

CHAPTER THREE

You Belong

Remember back to the days you spent playing on the schoolyard at recess or in Phys. Ed. class. All the kids would stand in anticipation, waiting to hear their names called as the team captains chose one by one the members of their team. They would first call out the names of the most popular kids, then the most athletic and capable, working their way down to the last two remaining.

Nobody wants to be picked last. It is one of the worst feelings for a kid and even an adult; to think that nobody wants you, that you don't belong. The feeling of rejection hurts, but we put on a brave face, pretend to be okay, and join in anyway.

As a kid my family moved every two years, all within the same town but just far enough away that I had to change schools. I always seemed to make friends rather quickly, and I enjoyed my various schools up until fifth grade. I would have to say that fifth and sixth grade were not the best experiences for me. It was an awkward age, and I was the new kid again. Even though I made many friends, I was still insecure. I wanted to have a close friend and true companion at my new school, like I'd had at my old school. There was a girl seated at the desk next to mine. I still remember her name and her face. I wanted to be her friend. One day I asked to borrow her lip balm, since girls that age often share such items. She obliged my request and handed it to me. After I had applied the lip balm, instead of handing it back to her I put it inside my own desk. I'm sure it looked like I was stealing it (I had planned on giving it back eventually), when in reality this was my attempt at solidifying our friendship. In my twelve-year-old mind I thought that if she let me keep *her* lip balm inside *my* desk, then we must be close friends, because that is what really close friends do, right? I quickly learned that I was mistaken. At recess she promptly told the other girls on the playground what I had done. I can still see them gathered in a circle, gossiping about the horror of it all. My heart was broken. After recess ended, we went back inside and took our seats, right next to each other. I immediately reached inside my desk, pulled out the lip balm and handed it back to its rightful owner. The desire to belong can make us do some ridiculous things. As we grow older this desire can even prompt us to engage in dangerous and harmful things.

Our choices and actions are often fueled by a desire to fit in, be accepted, and belong. This can lead to much regret and sorrow if in the process we lower our standards, bend our principles, or forget our morals—behaving in a way that is contrary to our identity as a child of God—just to get in with the "in crowd." In addition to this first response of trying to "fit in" there is a second response we often react with regarding the desire to belong: it is to withdraw or isolate as a means of self-protection, removing ourselves from the possibility of rejection. Satan, our enemy, loves when we choose either of these responses—the first leaves us open to sin and shame, the second gets us all alone where he can relentlessly prey on us. There is a third response though that our enemy never wants us to choose. It is one of confidence and security in who we really are—a member of God's family—standing firm against the lie that we don't belong.

I've had this discussion with women before and hurts from as far back as elementary and high school, and even more recent wounds are still fresh in our minds. Based on my previous encounters, I am pretty sure that many of you have experienced the feeling that you didn't belong at some point over the course of your life. There may be memories of things that you have done to try to "fit in," or times when you withdrew as a means of self-protection that are flashing through your mind right now. I encourage you to make up your mind to start choosing the third response of standing firm in the confidence that you are a child of God and the knowledge that you have a place of belonging with Jesus. Take your thoughts and feelings of insecurity captive and turn them over to God's Truth.

1. Describe a time when you felt that you didn't belong.

2. Have you ever done anything out of character in hopes of belonging? What did you do, and what was the result?

3. Have you ever withdrawn or isolated as a means of protecting yourself from rejection? Describe the situation.

4. Are you ready to work on choosing the third response? What will your first step be?

Knowing we belong to God and His holy family gives us the confidence we need, enabling us to never compromise our integrity just to please others and be accepted by them, and to never again isolate as a means of protection. We have a loving Father who accepts us as we are, who never excludes us, desires the best for us, and contrary to my classmates, He never gossips about us.

We all want to belong in some *way*, and to some *thing*. Families, teams, clubs, cliques, organizations, fraternities, sororities and gangs—these groups give us a place to come together with others who share common interests, purpose, passions and goals. They provide us with a place of belonging, they offer support, and they validate us as a person. It isn't surprising that we seek out these avenues of connection and belonging. God is the One who put this desire in our hearts, He never meant for us to be alone. We have been created for companionship and relationships. Being the loving Father that He is, He has provided a warm and loving place for you and me to belong. This place of belonging is open to everyone— it is the Family of God.

God chooses you! You are a member of His family and a valued player on His team!

Song of Solomon, 7:10, "I belong to my beloved, and his desire is for me."

Do you grasp the beauty of this verse? (We are going to spend more time studying the book *Song of Solomon* in a later chapter, but for now I wanted to share this verse with you.) God desires you; He wants you! You belong *to* Him, and you have a place of belonging *with* Him!

We don't have to be the fastest, smartest, most talented, or most fashionable. All that's needed for us to be accepted by God is that we receive Jesus Christ as our Lord and Savior. Based on His sacrifice for us, we are more than good enough. We are *amazing* in His sight! In fact, Jesus tells us to come as we are. He doesn't ask us to fit any mold before we come, He invites us to come to Him *as is*.

Child of God

Some may say that the following Old Testament verses of Isaiah apply only to Israel, but if we read Jesus' words found in the New Testament—John 5:24—we see that He considers all who believe in Him as Savior to be His true children, gaining eternal life with Him. So, let's claim these promises for ourselves, as descendants of Abraham (God's chosen patriarch of the faith, and the father of the nation of Israel), by faith in Jesus.

Isaiah 41:8-10, "But you, Israel, my servant, Jacob, whom I have chosen, you descendants of Abraham my friend, ⁹ I took you from the ends of the earth, from its farthest corners I called you. I said, 'You are my servant'; I have chosen you and have not rejected you. ¹⁰ So do not fear, for I am with you; do not be dismayed, for I am your God. I will strengthen you and help you; I will uphold you with my righteous right hand.'"

The word "rejection" may spark feelings of pain. Memories of rejection—from peers, the world around us, from supposed friends, our family, and even those who are expected to love and accept us the most, our parents—may surface in our minds all over again. Rejection can cause pain that makes our hearts truly hurt. Bitterness grows when we allow these wounds to fester in our hearts. Peace grows when we invite healing into our hearts, a healing that only the LORD can bring.

Let these words of the LORD sink in and bring the healing you need: "I called you," "I have chosen you and have not rejected you." Personally, when I read these words, I picture myself walking into a room full of people, scanning the scene hoping to find a friendly, welcoming face that would include me at their table. Then as I catch a glimpse of Jesus, His eyes lock on me, a warm smile spreads across His face, and

He calls me by name inviting me to sit at *His* table. He erases all my fears of rejection as He calls out, "Hey Tracy, come join me, I've saved a place just for you." Replace my name with yours and picture Jesus calling out to you, "Hey (your name here) _____, come join me. I've saved a place just for you." Jesus doesn't wait for us to ask if we can join Him, He takes the initiative and invites us to come.

Our Heavenly Father calls out to each of us from wherever we are, even "the ends of the earth." He knows your name and mine, and He calls to us. He beckons us to come to Him. We can come without fear of rejection; we come assuredly knowing that He has chosen us especially. He is our God who will strengthen and help us as His precious children.

5. Let's read the following verses to gain further assurance that we are indeed descendants of Abraham, by faith, and a child of God. Please note the affirmations found in each Scripture.

- **Galatians 3:7-9, 26-27**

- **Romans 9:8**

Chosen

We have just read further confirmation that we are God's child, not by being good enough, having the right pedigree, or earning our way, but just by placing our faith in Jesus Christ. Did you get that? Just by faith in the grace of God! The moment we believe in Him we immediately have a place in the family. Let's not forget that marvelous truth!

6. Please read **Ephesians 1:3-14** and underline all the words and phrases that clearly refer to our status of belonging.

   Ephesians 1:3-14, "Praise be to the God and Father of our Lord Jesus Christ, who has blessed us in the heavenly realms with every spiritual blessing in Christ. ^{4} For he chose us in him before the creation of the world to be holy and blameless in his sight. In love ^{5} he predestined us for adoption to sonship through Jesus Christ, in accordance with his pleasure and will— ^{6} to the praise of his glorious grace, which he has freely given us in the One he loves. ^{7} In him we have redemption through his blood, the forgiveness of sins, in accordance with the riches of God's grace ^{8} that he lavished on us. With all wisdom and understanding, ^{9} he made known to us the mystery of his will according to his good pleasure, which he purposed in Christ, ^{10} to be put into effect when the times reach their fulfillment—to bring unity to all things in heaven and on earth under Christ. ^{11} In him we were also chosen, having been predestined according to the plan of him who works out everything in conformity with the purpose of his will, ^{12} in order that we, who were the first to put our hope in

Christ, might be for the praise of his glory. ¹³ And you also were included in Christ when you heard the message of truth, the gospel of your salvation. When you believed, you were marked in him with a seal, the promised Holy Spirit, ¹⁴ who is a deposit guaranteeing our inheritance until the redemption of those who are God's possession—to the praise of his glory."

7. How do these Scriptures bring comfort to your heart?

8. Is this the first time you have considered Jesus as more than your way to salvation, but also as your way to a place of permanent belonging in His family? Explain.

I hope you noticed all the beautiful references to how God feels about you. He *chose* you and *adopted* you as His daughter through Jesus' sacrifice. Long before the world began, God had the perfect plan for making you, His child. Through Jesus you are included, for now and always. His Holy Spirit has marked you with His seal of belonging. You are His!

Isaiah 43:10, "'You are my witnesses,' declares the LORD, 'and my servant whom I have chosen, so that you may know and believe me and understand that I am he. Before me no god was formed, nor will there be one after me.'"

9. Our Sovereign, Almighty God is also our approachable and loving Father. According to **Isaiah 43:10** write the purpose for which God has chosen you. What does this mean?

God chose you with the purpose of inviting you to know Him intimately. He wants you to not just know *about* Him, but genuinely know Him as a Father. He wants you to trust, believe, and rely on the love He has for you. He wants you to truly grasp the fact that you belong to Him and understand that He is faithful by nature. He is the only true God; He is trustworthy; He is the God who was, and is, and always will be. He hangs in there with His family forever.

The Invitation

All are invited to belong in the Kingdom of God, but only those who accept the invitation and receive Jesus as Savior will be chosen to enter His family.

10. Please read **Matthew 22:1-14** and answer the following questions.

    a. In **verse 9** we see that God's invitation goes out to everyone. What is revealed about the heart of God as He continually reaches out to a needy world?

    b. What are the responses and excuses of those who refuse His invitation?

    c. Based on **verse 10**, we see that both the good and bad are invited. What does this reveal about our invitation into the Kingdom of God? Is it based on merit? How does this make you feel?

    d. During that period, a host would provide proper attire for all guests entering his banquet. In **verses 11-13** we see that someone has gotten into the party and is not wearing the wedding clothes that his host has offered. He has rejected the covering his host has required. This man is promptly excluded from the party. These verses confirm that we need Jesus. He is the One who clothes us in *His* righteousness, for *His* banquet. "For many are invited, but few are chosen" to stay and enjoy the blessings found in the Father's Presence. The Lord extends the invitation, we need only accept and put on the righteous clothing He's provided. Verse 4 details some of the extravagances that were prepared for those who accepted the king's invitation. What are some extravagances that the Lord has lavished on you?

11. Read the following verses for more insight on becoming a child of God. Note what you discover.

- **John 1:12**

- **Romans 8:14-15**

Call Me Father

The steps to becoming a full-fledged member of God's family are quite simple. Let's recap them: receive Jesus as Lord and Savior, place our faith in Him alone, become a child of God. And then we obey Him, not out of fear or obligation, not because we have to, but solely out of love. Why? Because "He first loved us." Our status of belonging is a done deal! We are adopted into His family, and adoption is always initiated by someone who dearly wants us to be their child. He is our Father, our Dad, our Daddy, our Papa, our Pappy.

12. You may have only ever pictured God as God, up in Heaven, distant and removed. How is your heart affected by the knowledge that God wants to be your Father?

Our response could be greatly impacted by the relationship we have with our earthly father. If he was (or is) loving, it will be easier for us to see our Heavenly Father the same way. If our earthly father was (or is) stern and harsh, our perception will be skewed, making it harder for us to view our Heavenly Father as gentle and kind. If he was emotionally distant, it may be harder to see our God as approachable and devoted. If our earthly father was altogether absent, it might be more difficult to trust God's faithfulness. This is exactly why it is so important to study the Bible and learn the truth about God. When we accurately know His character, our hearts and mouths will shout for joy! He is a Father like no other! The One who has adopted you and me is loving, gentle and kind, approachable and devoted, faithful and trustworthy! That deserves a shout of joy!

Psalm 105:43, "He brought out his people with rejoicing, His chosen ones with shouts of joy"

New Membership

There is indeed great joy as we embrace the fact that we belong to Jesus and the family—the church, the body, the Kingdom—of God. Because of that, we have canceled our membership to the world. We live according to our membership in the family of Christ. Along with the abundant blessings that come through our growing relationship with Jesus, there will be a distancing in our relationship to the world and all that it offers, and to what it says about what belonging means (because the world around us does have its own ideas as to what it means to belong). We now live according to our membership in His family, and we cancel our membership to the world in which we previously tried to fit in.

13. Please read the following verses and make note of what the Bible says regarding the transition from belonging to the world, to now belonging to Jesus—fitting in perfectly with Him.

- **John 15:18-20**

- 1 John 3:1

14. What does it mean to you personally to cancel your membership to the world, replacing it with a membership to God's family?

15. Had you ever considered that you must let go of the one in order to receive the other? How difficult is this for you?

16. Letting go of the "world", the things of our old life, will require effort; but God's Spirit, His Word—the Bible—prayer, and sincere godly friends will ease the process. You may have to say goodbye to old habits, old lifestyles, and even old friends, but God will replace whatever you let go of with something much better. What do you personally need to release?

17. The world is fickle, and its acceptance of us comes and goes depending on our performance, while the acceptance from God is secure and based on pure love. Does the unconditional acceptance from God make it easier to loosen your grip on the world?

Malachi 2:15, "Has not the one God made you? You belong to him in body and spirit."

Choosing Him

Every family has traits that are unique to it alone. The family of God is no different in that fact, but in many other ways it is very different than every other family on the planet. The character traits of God's family are based on His unchanging morals of Truth, His pure values, His unconditional love, and His command to forgive.

He chose us, we now choose Him and His ways daily in return.

18. Please read the following Psalms and note the things we now choose as God's chosen child.

- **Psalm 119:29-31**

- **Psalm 119:172-174**

Family

There are countless blessings that come from being in God's family. First of all, you get siblings—lots and lots of siblings! Now this may bring fear or excitement, depending on how functional or dysfunctional your earthly family is. Regardless, you now have more brothers and sisters than you can count, and in the grace of God alone, you can count *on* them. We receive the blessing of fellowship with brothers and sisters who have the same purpose, passions and goals as us—to love and glorify God! Remember back to the beginning of this chapter, the whole reason people join groups is to gather with those who share common goals, and interests, and have a place of belonging. Well, in the family of God we find this and more—we find people looking out for each other, helping each other, loving each other, praying for each other. **Keep in mind though, we are still just human, each one of us dealing with our own issues, so we need lots of help from the Holy Spirit to keep the unity that the family of God so deserves.** This is why it is so important that we mentally clothe ourselves in the humble attitude of Christ.

The family of God has a commonality which surpasses and covers over all the differences that seek to divide us—His name is Jesus. In Jesus there is no distinction between His family members—not background, heritage, race, gender, status, wealth, style, popularity, or power. We are all equal and one in Christ.

Colossians 3:10-11, "put on the new self, which is being renewed in knowledge in the image of its Creator. ¹¹ Here there is no Gentile or Jew, circumcised or uncircumcised, barbarian, Scythian, slave or free, but Christ is all, and is in all."

19. Even though we are *one*, our differences open the door for a lot of varying personalities, which is why God describes the need for a family dress code. Please read **Colossians 3:12-14** to see what we as God's chosen people are supposed to clothe ourselves in. Please list all the "garments" we are to put on.

20. Choosing Jesus daily means letting go of our selfish pride and having the same attitude as Christ. The clothes described in Colossians are actually just the attitudes that will help us to get along better and keep the unity with others in the family. Describe in your own words how these attitudes help in this way.

21. I know we often resort to depending on ourselves for everything, but let's see what the Bible has to say about some of the benefits of having each other to lean on. Please read the following Scriptures and make note of the exhortations and benefits God has for in store for His children.

- **Ecclesiastes 4:9-12**

- **Acts 2:32, 42-47**

- **Romans 12:10**

- **2 Corinthians 13:11-12**

- **2 Thessalonians 1:3**

- **Hebrews 10:23-25**

- **James 5:16**

- **1 John 4:12**

22. How are you doing when it comes to reaching out to others in the family of God for companionship? Allowing others to love you? Stepping outside yourself to help others? I realize it's scary to reach out and open ourselves up to others because we've been let down too many times before, but I hope that you will ask God to give you the courage to try again.

23. I want to acknowledge that the people in God's family don't always treat each other the way we should, but when the family of God *is functioning properly* it is the perfect example of humility and love in action. How have you experienced or witnessed the family of God coming together to encourage, support and love on each other?

I know without a doubt every one of you reading this study, and every woman walking this earth desires friendship. We may look around and think we are the only one on the outside looking in—the only one not connected in a special way. I have news for you, I have met many women who feel lonely and isolated and wish for a friend—even though they are part of the body of Christ. I want to share my story with you as a source of inspiration: When I began attending my current church over 20 years ago, I would quietly slip in, and take my seat in the back, often alone, and when service was over, I would collect my children and go home. Sure, I exchanged greetings with people, but it wasn't until *I made the effort* to connect that I started to feel I belonged. When I joined Bible Study, I came to know the names and faces of many others in my church. When I signed up to serve in ministry, I found others with common interests. I found friends. You may very well be thinking you already do all of this, but you still don't feel like you belong, or have any friends. Making friends sometimes takes repeated effort on our part—others may have their own self-protection shield up. Unfortunately, making friends isn't as instantaneous as it was in kindergarten; it takes time to build trust and relationships. Keep reaching out, there is someone out there who is waiting just for you.

To have a friend, you must also be a friend. It's a two-way street. In other words, friendship is an equal balance of give and take; it's a partnership. A true friend accepts your silliness, quirkiness, and even your crankiness—and you accept theirs. The most valuable friend is kind, thoughtful, and considerate, she welcomes you to be open and honest, and share your vulnerable heart with her—even when that calls for a little venting session. If you want this kind of friend, you must *be* this kind of friend. As much as you need a friend who is a good listener, your friend needs you to be a good listener for them—that sometimes means turning off your mouth and turning on your ears so you can hear what *they* are truly saying. Remember it's a give and take relationship which comes with bountiful benefits.

Years ago, *I prayed for friends,* and along with my effort to engage, God answered my prayers with some amazing women. Meeting with these women every week for the last 17 years and counting, along with a hearty dose of God's Word, has been the glue that helps keep my life intact.

If you desire a friend to do life with, I want you to take a moment to pray and ask God to bring a special Christian friend into your life for companionship, fellowship, fun, and support.

In the body of Christ, we should also be on the lookout for others who may need a friend and reach out to them. Take my word for it, there are many other women who feel just as vulnerable as you do and would love a friend. It's time for us to reach out and build each other up.

Philippians 2:3-4, "Do nothing out of selfish ambition or vain conceit. Rather, in humility value others above yourselves, ⁴ not looking to your own interests but each of you to the interests of the others."

24. Have you made an effort to get plugged into your local church? Is there a women's ministry you could get involved in? I have found that one of the best ways to overcome the insecurity of belonging is to get involved in a serving capacity at the church you attend. (Remember that to get connected you actually have to show up.)

25. Had you ever considered asking God to send you a friend?

26. Have you ever considered what it means for you to be a good friend to others? How can you be a better friend?

Always and Everywhere

One major difference found in the family of God is its eternal existence, and worldwide span.

God's family reaches far and wide. You can travel to the other side of the planet and still encounter a family member. You may come across someone you have never met before, but the moment you realize they are also a believer in Jesus Christ is the moment you realize you have an everlasting, eternal bond. You have found another sister or brother in Christ.

I have been in quite a few church services where we have had a guest speaker from a faraway land, a distant country, with foreign customs, and a different language, yet the moment they open their mouth in praise and prayer—even if I can't understand a word they are saying—my heart leaps as our spirits are joined in unity of worship, love, and the family of God.

27. Have you ever experienced this familial bond with strangers before? When and where?

28. Again, I emphasize that when the family of God is *functioning as it should*—loving, compassionate, understanding, and kind—it not only feels different to those who belong to it, but it looks different to the world around us. Please read the following verses and make note of the encouragements and commands for us as children of God.

- **1 John 5:18-19**

- **Philippians 2:14-16**

- **John 13:34-35**

29. What are some specific ways you have seen the family of God differ from the world around you?

God's family is not exclusive in any way, shape, or form; His family is all-inclusive and has room for everyone who receives and believes in the gift of God. Let's hold out the hope of belonging to a world full of rejection. Gaining confidence in our sense of belonging isn't only for the purpose of making us feel better; with it comes the purpose of including others as well.

In closing, the world will try to convince us to compromise ourselves in order to fit in, but our Heavenly Father calls us to never compromise who we are, standing firm and unwavering in our identity as His beloved child. It's time we start believing that we belong to Someone and something really amazing!

The Simple Truth: You Belong!

A Simple Prayer: Dear Heavenly Father, thank You for adopting me into Your Family and giving me a secure place of eternal belonging. Whenever I start to feel insecure, like I don't "fit in," help me to remember Your Words and gain confidence from knowing that I always belong with You. Amen.

CHAPTER FOUR

You Matter

Have you ever felt as if you had no voice? Have you ever felt ignored, misunderstood, like your words fell on deaf ears, that your opinion didn't matter, or that no one cared to hear the cries of your heart? Have you ever raised your voice in hopes of getting someone to hear you, or just stopped talking because you knew no one was listening?

Have you ever felt invisible, like others looked right through you, felt you were insignificant, or that you didn't matter?

Such feelings lead to insecurity and hopelessness. It is imperative for us to know someone cares, know that we are significant, that we are seen and heard, and that our lives are validated in someone else's eye.

Matthew 10:29-31, "'Are not two sparrows sold for a penny? Yet not one of them will fall to the ground outside your Father's care. ³⁰And even the very hairs of your head are all numbered.³¹ So don't be afraid; you are worth more than many sparrows.'"

Our Heavenly Father cares deeply about you! No detail of your life escapes His knowledge. He sees when your heart is breaking and the pain is leaking out, and His heart weeps for you. He sees when your heart is overflowing with abundant joy, and you feel as though you could leap ten feet in the air, and He rejoices with you. Scripture says He knows every hair on your head. He pays great attention to everything about you. You matter! You are significant! You are seen! You are heard!

Throughout this chapter you will notice an underlying theme of prayer is present in each of the individuals' stories we will study. Prayer is the act of communicating with a God who hears you.

Psalm 116:1, "I love the LORD, for he heard my voice; he heard my cry for mercy."

The Bible is filled with countless stories of individuals just like us, who prayed for God to see and hear their cries for mercy, for His help and intervention. God heard and answered them in powerful ways. Elizabeth and Zechariah earnestly prayed for a child and were blessed to parent John the Baptist. Joshua prayed for more hours in the day so he could fight the battle before him, and God held the sun still in the sky. The Psalms are filled with David's heartfelt prayers, his cries for the LORD to see him and pour out His mercy. The Psalms are also filled with David's prayers of thanksgiving, as he recounts all the ways that God had listened and answered his cries.

1. How do these examples encourage you to bring your own heart's desire before the LORD?

I personally have cried out to the LORD on different occasions, and for various reasons. Regardless of how and when my prayers are answered, I know without a doubt God hears every one of them, and answers according to His perfect will, because I matter to Him.

He hears every one of your prayers too.

Seen and Heard

Let's look at a special story found in Genesis about a woman who seemed to have no voice of her own. As we'll see, everyone else made decisions for her. *Her* needs were overlooked, and *her* desires didn't seem to matter.

2. Please read **Genesis 16:1-15** and answer the following questions.

    a. What thoughts come to mind as you read part one of Hagar's story?

    b. How did Abram and Sarai treat/mistreat Hagar?

    c. What decisions were being made for Hagar?

    d. How do you think she felt?

    e. How did Hagar respond to this disregard and abuse?

f. Where did the angel find Hagar? What were his instructions to her?

g. Record the angel's words of comfort and encouragement. What promises did the angel deliver?

h. After her encounter with the angel, what name does Hagar ascribe to the LORD?

i. How were her eyes opened to the LORD? What does she say about her own "vision" of Him?

Regardless of what brought Hagar to this point—whether the actions of others, or attitudes of her own—she now found herself in need of some serious Divine intervention.

Hagar's opinion was silenced. Others made decisions for her, never consulting her over the course of her own life. She was overlooked and abandoned by everyone who knew her, but God never lost sight of her. He heard her cries of misery and sent an angel to come to her aid. Our cries never fall on deaf ears either; God's ears and eyes are always attentive to our needs. However, it is not enough for God to see us. We must open our eyes to *see Him*, and recognize, and *believe* that He sees us. Great confidence comes and equips us to face life when this realization occurs within us.

After being visited by the angel, Hagar, in faith and obedience to the LORD, returned to the household of Abraham (Abram) and Sarah (Sarai). Hagar gave birth to her son and named him Ishmael as the LORD had directed. Over time—13-14 years later—Abraham and Sarah were blessed with a child of their own, and named him Isaac, also according to the LORD's will. As the story of Hagar continues, we see that she is still an overlooked woman, and her son is seen as insignificant as well.

3. Please read part two of Hagar's story, found in **Genesis 21:8-21** and answer the corresponding questions.

    a. What thoughts come to mind as you read part two of Hagar's story?

b. Had anything changed in Hagar's circumstances? Was she being treated any differently?

c. We see that Hagar once again found herself abandoned and alone in the desert, but this time with her son Ishmael. Imagine how hopeless she must have felt as she looked at her situation, and how her heart must have broken for her precious son. Reflect and write a description of the relief she must have felt, as once again an angel of the LORD was sent to her rescue.

d. In **verses 21:17** we are told twice "God heard the boy crying." What comfort does this bring regarding your own tears?

e. What words of comfort did the angel give to Hagar about her son?

f. What blessing was revealed as God opened her eyes? Do you notice the significance in that it wasn't until her eyes were opened that she was able to see the blessing right beside her?

g. Are you aware of the blessings—despite circumstances—that God has surrounded you with? If so, list them. If you're not yet aware, ask Him to open your eyes, mind, and heart—to see, receive, and appreciate what is right around you.

h. How has God worked, and where have you seen His hand move in your life?

Although it seemed like all hope was lost, and circumstances were too much to bear, God heard the cries of both Hagar and her son. God never left them and was providing for them all along amid their circumstances. God gave them promises of hope for the future and promises they could cling to for that very moment. Just like Hagar we must *choose* to believe the promises God gives to us. Also, like Hagar, and the well of fresh water right beside her, our eyes must open in order for us to notice the blessings of God's action and provision all around us.

The eyes of the LORD are always on us, and He continually provides for our needs—just not always the way we would plan or expect. So be on the lookout for your blessings.

Prayers Received

4. As you read this collection of Psalms write out each verse and record your thoughts regarding each. Let these become personal prayers to the LORD in your time of need.

- **Psalm 4:1**

- **Psalm 34:7**

- **Psalm 6:9**

- **Psalm 17:6**

- **Psalm 66:20**

- **Psalm 141:2**

2 Chronicles 16:9, "For the eyes of the LORD range throughout the earth to strengthen those whose hearts are fully committed to him."

5. According to **2 Chronicles 16:9**, for what purpose does the LORD search the earth?

Swift Replies

6. The Psalms we just read make it very clear God hears, receives, and acts on our prayers. Please read **Daniel 9:20-23** and watch the proclamations of the Psalms come to life in this story of Daniel.

    a. What was Daniel doing?

    b. What was God's response?

    c. What did the angel say to Daniel?

    d. How do you feel knowing that God acts on your prayers?

I hope you noticed that while Daniel was still in the process of praying, God sent His angel—His messenger Gabriel—in answer to his prayers. While the words of prayer were still on Daniels lips, God had responded with action. God doesn't put our prayers in a stack on His desk, and say He'll get to them later. He doesn't pretend to be listening while His mind is elsewhere. Our prayers matter to God. We matter to God. He is attentive to our needs and desires.

Daniel 9:23, "As soon as you began to pray, a word went out, which I have come to tell you, for you are highly esteemed."

Although Daniel's prayers were answered immediately and dramatically in this instance, we mustn't get discouraged if ours aren't answered in the same exact way. Of course, we'd prefer for God to respond this way every time, but in His sovereignty, He often doesn't. We must remember that His ways and timing are best, despite what we think or feel. This is where faith and trust come in—we must believe that God is good, and that we matter to Him greatly. He sees the past, present, and future, and all the details going on behind the scenes that we don't. So, we need to trust His judgment and His response to our prayers. He might not change our situations the way we'd like, but He can change our hearts and equip us to face our challenges.

Never Out of Reach

If you ever think you've wandered too far from God for Him to hear you, or that your situation is beyond hope, think again. Let's look at someone who rebelled against God and appeared to be in an extremely hopeless situation.

7. Please read these snippets from the story of Jonah and describe the scene. **Jonah 1:1-3; 2:1-2, 10**

    a. What is Jonah's mindset in **verses 1:1-3**? How is this reflected in his actions?

    b. Have you ever run away from something you knew God wanted you to do? If so, did you feel like God would reject your prayers if you reached out to Him?

    c. Does God's attentiveness and mercy in response to Jonah's prayers surprise you? Why?

    d. Reflect on and express any comfort or confidence this example of Jonah gives you.

We see that God gave Jonah specific instructions to follow, but Jonah decided not to obey God and was in fact running away, trying to hide from God. In the process, he got himself into a lot of trouble. Jonah in his desperate situation called out for God's help and mercy. Contrary to what we might expect—that God would leave Jonah where he deserved to be—God responded and gave him much better than he merited. God heard Jonah and saved him from the pit of death and restored him to life.

And in the same way, God always gives *us* much better than what we deserve; He is willing to rescue us from our rebellion and restore our lives too.

From the story of Jonah, it becomes very clear that we are never too far gone, we are never too hopeless, and we are never beyond God's reach. His eyes are always on us. Our rebellion doesn't cancel out the love and care that God has for us. He waits for us to turn from our rebellion and call out to Him. He is faithful to respond to us. He reaches for us in the very depths of our sin and disobedience and delivers us out of it. Jonah was confident of the LORD's character as he prayed from the belly of a fish, under the surface of the ocean, in the grip of death.

"In my distress I called to the LORD, and He answered me. From deep in the realm of the dead I called for help, and you listened to my cry." Jonah 2:2

Hopefully Jonah's story fills you with confidence too. Always remember that you are never too far from God for Him to reach you.

No matter where you are, no matter what you've done, you matter to God.

Jesus, Our Example

Jesus, our perfect example, prayed to the Father, knowing that His prayers were heard. He prayed often—with others, and in solitary. He prayed with thanksgiving in all situations. Jesus knew that when His soul was overwhelmed with sorrow, it was time to pray. He was confident that His Heavenly Father heard His prayers, saw His heart, and had the capability to respond with power.

8. Please read the following Scriptures and record your insights into Jesus' prayer life.

- **Luke 5:16**

- **Matthew 14:19-21**

- **Mark 14:32-36**

- **Luke 22:39-46**

a. Why did Jesus pray? What was His underlying motive?

b. How does Jesus describe the Father in **Mark 14:32-36**?

c. What were His exhortations to the disciples? Why did He encourage them to pray?

With Jesus as their example, the disciples knew the importance of prayer, and it was the one thing they asked Him to teach them—how to pray.

Luke 11:1, "One day Jesus was praying in a certain place. When he finished, one of his disciples said to him, 'Lord, teach us to pray, just as John taught his disciples.'"

Jesus introduced them to a new way of prayer, of calling out to their Abba, Father, who is both powerful *and approachable*. He is not far off, uninvolved, and uninterested; on the contrary, our God is very near, very involved, and exceedingly interested in every aspect of our lives. Mark recorded how Jesus prayed before He went to the cross: *"Abba*, Father," He said, "Everything is possible for you." (Mark 14:36) Jesus led as our example of faith and confidence, affirming the absolute Truth that God the Father sees, hears, and cares about all our prayers.

He Seeks Us

In **1 Kings 19:3-13,** we find the story of Elijah. He was coming off a great victory. He had just personally experienced the power of God; God had helped him miraculously defeat the pagan god Baal, and hundreds of his priests and prophets. Elijah should have been feeling confident at this point, but instead, overcome with fear, he was running for his life. He felt alone and was ready to give up completely. The faithfulness and miraculous power of God had quickly been forgotten. Elijah had taken his eyes off God, but God had not taken His eyes off Elijah.

9. Please read **1 Kings 19:3-13** and answer the following questions.

    a. What do **verses 19:4, 10** reveal about Elijah's mindset? What are his exact words regarding his situation?

b. How does God use the angel to meet Elijah's needs while he is in the wilderness, waiting to die?

c. Please notice that in **verse 19:4**, Elijah "prayed that he might die." There are some prayers that God does not answer the way we'd like. It's not because we don't matter, but the exact opposite—we do matter, and He wants the best for us. What thoughts come to mind?

d. Once Elijah retreats to the cave how does God reach out to him?

e. What is God's question to him?

f. Do you recognize the gentle way God encourages Elijah to regain his confidence? How does this speak to you?

g. When we take our eyes off God, we quickly forget His past faithfulness and power in our own lives. What steps can you take to make sure you keep focused on Him and keep living in the victory He has achieved for you?

As we see, Elijah was overwhelmed and ready to give up on life. He ran away and retreated to a cave all by himself, saying these words, "I have had enough, LORD." God sought him out and spoke to him in a gentle whisper saying, "What are you doing here?" God knew that with His mighty help Elijah had just experienced a great victory and asks why he has now run off in fear, when he should still be living in confidence.

The same is true of us—we may have experienced the mighty, miraculous power of God in our own lives, but the moment life gets hard, we too get discouraged, lose focus, give up, and run away in defeat, but

God relentlessly seeks us out. Why? Because we matter to Him. He doesn't always come with loud, rumbling, forceful power. He often comes in quiet tenderness, which we desperately need in our moment of weakness. He doesn't rebuke us. He calmly and lovingly asks us, *what are you doing here (insert your name) _____? Why are you running away from life, and from Me? You have seen My power. You have felt my love. Let's get back out there together. You and Me, forever.*

Dear friend, don't ever run from God, instead run straight towards Him. Let His gentle whispers fill you with confidence. Listen to His voice and let it drown out your fears, feel the brush of His hand as it wipes away your silent tears. My dear, may God remind you that He is always, always, always, very, very, near.

Dandelion Prayers

A silly excitement bubbles up inside me whenever I come across a Dandelion. To me it's a flower that represents hope. When I was a child, I made wishes on them, but through the years I have come to make prayers on them. You see there is a big difference between wishes and prayers: wishes blow aimlessly in the wind while our prayers are carried on the wings of angels into the throne room of God Almighty. Each time I hold a Dandelion between my fingers, I marvel at how something can be so simple, yet so wondrously complex at the same time. And as I reflect on the fact that God made this precious flower, I am filled with hope and confidence. I take a deep breath in, fill my cheeks with air, and blow out with a powerful whoosh. I then watch as the tiny, white, cottony puffs float effortlessly up toward the heavens, whisking my thanksgiving, cares, and prayers upward to God, who receives it all.

The Bible uses other descriptions of our prayers reaching God in His throne room.

Revelation 5:8, "Each one had a harp and they were holding golden bowls full of incense, which are the prayers of God's people."

Revelation 8:2-4, "And I saw the seven angels who stand before God, and seven trumpets were given to them. ³ Another angel, who had a golden censer, came and stood at the altar. He was given much incense to offer, with the prayers of all God's people, on the golden altar in front of the throne. ⁴ The smoke of the incense, together with the prayers of God's people, went up before God from the angel's hand."

    10. Have you ever considered that your prayers are a delight to the LORD, that they are described as incense, a pleasing aroma ascending before the throne?

11. As you reflect over this chapter, whose story most resonates with your heart? Hagar, Daniel, Jonah, Jesus, the disciples, or Elijah? Which response of God encourages you most at this time?

Always and Everything

Ephesians 6:18, "And pray in the Spirit on all occasions with all kinds of prayers and requests. With this in mind, be alert and always keep on praying for all the Lord's people."

1 Thessalonians 5:17, "pray continually"

Whatever burden is weighing on your heart, whatever joy brings a smile to your face, pray about it! God's ears and eyes are attentive to every detail of your life. You can share your burden and joy here:

Like the Birds

As I sit outside on the back patio this morning enjoying my hot cup of hazelnut coffee, I notice a wide variety of cheery birds flitting around. They fly and hop from tree to tree, and bush to bush; they skitter around in the dirt, nibbling on the bits of seed they find. They sing and chirp with delight as they let the golden sunshine warm their feathery little bodies. As I observe their morning activity a curious thought comes to mind... They have not a care in the world (except maybe a wild cat or hawk to be on guard against.) Their needs are provided for every morning. I seriously doubt that they lie in their nests at night, kept awake with stress and worry the way we humans do. Can you imagine the momma bird making lists in her mind of all the things she will need to accomplish the following day? Can you imagine her saying to herself, "Let's see, I have to get up early, gather more twigs to freshen the nest, go find worms and get back to the nest before the children awake, make sure I chew the worms well before feeding my babies..." Can you imagine her letting worry about the future overwhelm her as she tries to settle into that elusive sleep and rest? Can you imagine her letting worrisome thoughts run rampant in her mind, thinking something like this, "What if I oversleep? What if I can't find any twigs or worms? What if one of the kids gets sick? What if they don't catch onto this whole flying thing? What will I do when they grow up and leave the nest? What will I do if they never grow up and leave the nest?" Yes, I seriously doubt that any of these thoughts overwhelm them at night. It's time to take a lesson from the birds and get a good night's rest. Worrying about tomorrow only steals precious time and joy from today. As our head hits the pillow each night it's a very good idea to remind ourselves of and thank God for all His care and provision of that day. We would also be wise to find comfort and peace in handing over all the cares and concerns for the day to come; handing them over to our Heavenly Father who never sleeps and continually watches over us. Don't worry, you matter to God.

Through prayer and petition lay your concerns before the LORD, and then trust Him with your life and all that's entailed.

Psalm 4:8, "I will lie down and sleep in peace, for you alone, O LORD, make me dwell in safety."

Matthew 6:25-27, "'Therefore I tell you, do not worry about your life, what you will eat or drink; or about your body, what you will wear. Is not life more than food, and the body more than clothes? 26 Look at the birds of the air; they do not sow or reap or store away in barns, and yet your heavenly Father feeds them. Are you not much more valuable than they? 27 Can any one of you by worrying add a single hour to your life?'"

The Simple Truth: You Matter!

A Simple Prayer: Dear God, thank You for seeing me and hearing me. Help me to gain confidence in knowing that I matter to You, and that You care about every detail of my life—the big and the small. May I turn to You and not pull away. May I seek You with all my heart and never stray. Thank You for Your unending faithfulness to me. Amen.

"'Because he loves me,' says the LORD, 'I will rescue him; I will protect him, for he acknowledges my name. He will call on me, and I will answer him;

I will be with him in trouble, I will deliver him and honor him.

With long life I will satisfy him and show him my salvation.'"

Psalm 91:14-16

Recount times that the Lord has heard your prayers and acted on your behalf. Take a moment to praise Him for His timely response. You can also use this space to pour out your heart and ask Him to answer and deliver you now:

CHAPTER FIVE

You are Beautiful

When God made the birds and fish, He said, "It is good." When He made the animals of the land, He said, "It is good." When he placed the stars, moon, and sun in the heavens, He said, "It is good." When He made you, a smile of great pleasure spread across His face, and He said, "It is very good." God doesn't make mistakes. He made you just the way you are, special and unique, unlike anyone else. Let God's words sink into your heart and mind and give you the encouragement and confidence to be uniquely YOU today.

Genesis 1:31, "God saw all that he had made, and it was very good."

1. Knowing that you are one of God's creations, what is your reaction to the fact that God said all His creation, "is good?" Do you believe that He calls *you* His "good" creation? Is this easy or difficult for you to accept?

2. Do you believe that God doesn't make mistakes? (Just for the record, He doesn't. Ever.) What personal experiences have led to your opinion?

3. We are often harsh and critical of ourselves, noticing every flaw, wishing to be different. Before we proceed any further, I would like to pause for a moment, with the purpose of having you pray and ask the LORD to help you accept whole-heartedly that *you* are His "good creation," just the way you are.

Unique

Our world is filled with awe-inspiring beauty. Everywhere we look, something new, majestic, beautiful, and special catches our eye. God's creation is amazing because it is always unique, always intriguing. Even in the simplest of creations, we find great complexity. God is the Ultimate Artist, paying close attention to the intricate and delicate details of His work. From mere observation, we may not notice the minute distinctions of His creation, but upon closer investigation we find that each one is exceptionally unique.

Let me explain: If we took a trip to the zoo, we may see giraffes or zebras which, from our vantage point—safely behind the fence—appear to look alike. All the giraffes are tall, with long necks, long legs, and brown spots covering their bodies. Did you know that the spots of each giraffe are unrepeated? No two are alike in all of creation. The same is true of the zebra's stripes. In all of creation no two zebras have the same exact pattern. Let's look at snowflakes—have you ever caught a snowflake on your tongue? Out of all the countless tiny white flakes that fall from the sky, not one is identical to another. God used the same creativity when He made you. There is only one of you. Your fingerprints are exclusive to you alone, different from every other person who has ever lived. God doesn't make cookie-cutter creations. Something is valued as special because it is rare. Consider a beautiful portrait hanging on the walls of a museum; it is counted as priceless because it is a one-of-a-kind masterpiece. All reproductions of the original pale in comparison. The rarity and originality of the artist's work is what constitutes its value.

God has a reason for making you exactly the way you are. You are uniquely created by Him. You are a priceless masterpiece!

Trying to fit the mold of what the world deems perfect—wearing a certain size or brand of jeans, or wearing your hair just so—doesn't make you special. Being who God made *you* to be makes *you* special.

You are still an individual even if you have an *identical* twin. God does not lump you both together. You are each unique, distinct, and special in His eyes.

I have taken the liberty of researching the definition of a couple words pertaining to your specialness. The following definitions are according to Merriam-Webster.com:

- **Individuality:** Total character peculiar to and distinguishing an individual from others; separate or distinct existence; individual; person
- **Originality:** the quality or state of being original; fresh of aspect, design or style; the power of independent thought or constructive imagination

You are an individual, and an original. You are a priceless work of art! Our Heavenly Father created you in a very specific way. He knit you together, stitch-by-stitch, with *unique* characteristics, traits, qualities, personality, gifts, talents, appearance, and even quirks, to make the remarkable and complete package of you.

4. Please read **Psalm 139:13-16** and answer the following questions.

Psalm 139:13-16, "For you created my inmost being; you knit me together in my mother's womb. ¹⁴I praise you because I am fearfully and wonderfully made; your works are wonderful, I know that full well. ¹⁵My frame was not hidden from you when I was made in the secret place, when I was woven together in the depths of the earth. ¹⁶Your eyes saw my unformed body; all the days ordained for me were written in your book before one of them came to be."

a. What about these verses stands out/touches you most?

b. What two *needlework terms* are used to describe the way God created you?

c. What two words describe how you were *made*? **(139:14)**

d. Do you know "full well," that all of God's works—including you—are wonderful?

e. Who was watching over you while you were in your mother's womb? **(139:15-16)**

f. When did God become aware of you? Had He planned on you? **(139:16)**

g. Are you beginning to realize the tender care that God put into creating you? How does this speak to your heart?

Based on these Scriptures, it is obvious that you are no accident. God planned you long before the world began. He had every precise detail of you sketched out in His mind. Long before the technology of ultrasound gave insight to the eyes of doctors and parents, your Heavenly Father—the only One who saw you in the quiet, isolated safety of your mother's womb—lovingly formed you, as He carefully knit and wove you together. You are one of God's "works," and His works are "wonderful." I hope you are coming to believe that "full well."

According to Biblehub.com, the NAS Exhaustive Concordance finds the Hebrew root meaning of the word **"wonderfully"**: to be separated or distinct; distinguished; make a distinction; set apart; wonderfully, wondrously show—that's YOU! You are *wonderfully* made!

Beautiful (im)Perfections

Scripture tells us we are beautiful, but do we always believe it? If you're anything like me, this may have been a struggle and a cause of insecurity at times. As a toddler I had beautiful, soft, blonde curls. Throughout elementary school my sweet curls grew into long, golden brown waves. I wore my hair in ponytails, pig tails, buns, and often it just flowed loosely down my back. Well, my beautiful hair lasted until I hit the middle school years, when it decided to turn frizzy, unruly, and just plain huge! At one point, I begged my mom to use the thinning shears on my hair with hopes of taming it down, but this only made it grow bigger. I then resorted to a new plan of attack against my out-of-control locks. I began the routine of pulling my hair back into a ponytail and continued wrapping more bands all the way down to the ends. I would then place a winter snow cap on my head, all with the purpose of flattening my hair. This is how I went to bed at night, hoping to wake up with silky, smooth hair. Needless to say, it didn't work the way I had hoped. Thanks to modern hair products I am better equipped to make the best of my curls. I have come to appreciate the hair that God gave me, and I wouldn't think of trading it for anything different.

5. What areas of your appearance do you most struggle with? Which things cause the most insecurity?

6. Have you ever done anything strange—like wearing a hat to bed—to impact your looks? Did it work the way you planned?

7. Over time have you come to accept and appreciate yourself as you are? Or is this a current struggle? Explain.

What we see as imperfections, are just unique beauty. God made you and me. He doesn't make mistakes; He creates incomparable beauty in each of us.

It's time to make peace with yourself and begin appreciating the way God made you.

Ecclesiastes 3:11, "He has made everything beautiful in its time. He has also set eternity in the human heart; yet no one can fathom what God has done from beginning to end."

Beautiful Variety

My life is blessed by many amazing women. My family is filled with women who have helped make me who I am today—my mom, both of my grandmas, my sisters, my stepmom, my mother-in-law, my sisters-in-law, my aunts, my cousins, my nieces. Each has contributed to my life in their own special way. I have many dear friends, including some I've had since childhood and whom I share many memories with. I have a group of precious women that I meet with week after week in Bible study. They are all unique.

Whenever I sit in my backyard, surrounded by my beautiful flowers, I am reminded of each of the lovely women in my life. As my gaze wanders around the yard my eyes land on the flowers one by one; each is unique and beautiful in its own special way.

There are the robust, pink ones, full and bright; the petite, cheery, orange tinted ones; the white, delicate blooms; the tight yellow buds still waiting to blossom. There is a pale lavender one hiding amid them all. Each flower has its own color, shape, size, and fragrance. God in His creative sovereignty made them each uniquely different, but all equally beautiful. My hope is that every dear woman, some I know, others I may never meet, would come to celebrate her own beauty, to realize her own worth just as she is, not comparing herself to the woman next to her. I hope that she loves and accepts herself just the way she has been created. I am so glad that God has put a variety of flowers in my yard, and I am so very glad that He has put a wide variety of women in my life. Each is a beautiful blessing to me in her own special way.

8. Do you see why variety is so beautiful? Do you notice the unique beauty in others? In yourself? Explain.

9. True beauty doesn't come in a "one size, shape, or color fits all." Have you ever tried to fit the mold of what society—via magazines, movies, commercials, etc.—pushes on women? How does this standard affect you, if at all?

Makeover by Jesus

Each of us is beautiful in our own unique way. God took some standard features and changed them ever so slightly, making them distinct on each of us. Our eyes, nose, mouth, ears, skin tone, cheekbones, forehead, chin, body shape and size are what make us physically look the way we do. God put all the pieces together and made you and me. He is well pleased with the way He made us.

Whatever physical appearance God has given you, know that you are beautiful.

God is the One who created us to look a certain way; but there are ways we greatly affect our own beauty. I'm not talking about makeup, face lifts, clothes, jewelry, or anything like that. I'm talking about our attitude. Yes, our appearance is greatly impacted by our attitude!
Have you ever noticed how the most physically attractive woman can instantly become ugly if her attitude and behavior are rude, harsh, or obnoxious? Or how a woman with a plainer appearance instantly becomes stunningly beautiful in your eyes, as she exhibits kindness, gentleness, and grace? True beauty radiates from the inside.

As we walk with the Lord, the countenance of our face changes, reflecting the beauty of Jesus to those around us. We are even more beautiful as He shines through us; we are beautiful with an unfading beauty that weathers the storms and is unaffected by age over the years. True beauty comes from deep within. As kindness, gentleness, goodness, and more overflow in our lives we become more beautiful. Jesus is the One who softens the lines of our face, unfurrows our brow, removes our scowl, replacing them with a glimmer in our eyes, a rosiness to our cheeks, and an upward curve at the edges of our mouths. Jesus is the Master at complete makeovers…. inside and out.

10. Have you ever had the experience of watching someone transform before your eyes (for better or worse), just because they opened their mouth or acted in a certain way? Explain.

11. Have you ever met someone who radiated beauty from the inside out? Someone that glowed and shined because of her relationship with Jesus? Describe this person.

12. Please read the following verses and record what you learn about true beauty.

- **1 Peter 3:3**

- **Colossians 3:12**

- **Proverbs 31:30**

- **Proverbs 16:31**

- **1 Timothy 2:9-10**

Scripture is not saying you shouldn't put effort into your appearance, or that wearing a nice outfit, or a necklace is bad. Scripture is just warning us to get our priorities straight, by being more concerned with the things that make us beautiful from the inside-out. Our attitude and our character do more to affect our beauty than any make-up could possibly do. When you're getting dressed in the morning be sure to put on (clothe) yourself with the attitude of Jesus.

13. How do these descriptions compare to the world's view of beauty? How do they compare to your view of beauty?

I'm sure you've noticed that the Word of God flips the world's understanding of beauty completely upside-down. The world tries to convince us that beauty is *only* found in youth, and glamour, and perfection; it says that beauty should be flaunted—on obvious display for all the world to see, with overly-revealing clothing—as a means of attracting attention. Instead, God tells us that beauty, value, dignity, and worth are found in every life, no matter the stage or age, shape or size. It is found in our attitude, and we don't have to fight the aging process, but instead embrace it. Gray hair is a symbol of beauty, a symbol of wisdom. Wrinkles are, quite simply, glorious lines etched into faces from both sorrow and joy, telling the story of a life well-lived. God finds beauty in a *quiet and gentle spirit*, in *modesty*, in *wisdom*, in *righteousness,* in *kindness and compassion*. Ask God to give you His perspective on true beauty. His kind of beauty stands the test of time; it isn't a fad or fashion that comes and goes out of style at a moment's notice.

Your best accessory is a warm and genuine smile.

Altogether Beautiful

Song of Songs 4:7, "You are altogether beautiful, my darling; there is no flaw in you."

There are a few interpretations as to the meaning of the book "Song of Songs." Most scholars agree that the book encapsulates the passionate relationship between a bridegroom—King Solomon—and his bride. The Scriptures are also said to reveal the beauty and sanctity of marriage between every husband and wife in God's eyes. Another interpretation serves as an allegory of the LORD's love for the nation of Israel. For our purposes here it will represent a message of Christ's love for His bride—the church, as a whole—and for each of us individually. This narrative recounts the story of Christ's love, how He has sought after us, wooed us, captivated us, and has drawn us into an everlasting relationship with Himself. The book is filled, from beginning to end, with generous compliments and praises of our King toward us.

14. Please read through the book of **Song of Songs (Song of Solomon)**—yes, **the complete 8 chapters**— and answer the following questions. **Take special note of verses 1:15; 4:1, 7, 9; 6:4; 7:6.** All the parts spoken by the *Lover* are the king referring to his beloved wife.

a. I realize that the language may differ from what we're normally used to hearing, but does the description of such expressive and extravagant love cause you to blush? Why?

b. Since this story is a picture of God's feelings about you, how do you feel knowing that you take God's breath away?

c. How do you respond to attention from others? Does it make you uncomfortable? Do you deflect attention onto other people?

d. How well do you receive compliments? Do you easily and graciously accept? Do you disregard them? Do you belittle yourself in a serious, or joking way, in response?

Every page in the book "Song of Songs" is filled with unbridled descriptions of the bride's beauty—from head to toe—and expressions of the king's adoration for her. The king is enthralled with his bride. Within eight short chapters, he calls her beautiful eight times.

This is how God feels about you!

Love Yourself

In **Matthew 22:37-38,** Jesus was asked which were the greatest commands for us to follow, and *"Jesus replied: 'Love the Lord your God with all your heart and with all your soul and with all your mind. ³⁸ This is the first and greatest commandment. ³⁹ And the second is like it: Love your neighbor as yourself.'"*

In most commentaries and sermons, the *love for God* and *for our neighbor* are highlighted in this exchange, and with good reason—these are the commands that Jesus has given us to follow, and from which all godly living will flow. But I have found there to be an often overlooked, underlying theme: Jesus said we are to love our neighbors *as ourselves*, which brings with it the assumption that we indeed *love ourselves*. I think it's sometimes easier for us to appreciate and love others, than it is to even tolerate ourselves. We look at others and think, she's so pretty, so kind, so talented, so organized...and so on. Do we ever apply these gracious, generous thoughts to ourselves? It's about time we start showing ourselves some grace, and begin seeing *ourselves* as special, instead of being our own worst critic. From now on let's determine to conquer our negative self-image, raise our low self-esteem, replace our negative self-talk, stop being overly self-conscious, and cease trying to be someone else!

Let's make a clean break from focusing on our flaws and imperfections, and just appreciate who and how God has made us to be.

15. I know for many of you this next assignment will be excruciatingly painful—like pulling teeth—but I would like you to **make a list of everything that makes you special**. This is not considered bragging about yourself; this is bragging on God's "good creation." List as many things as you can. Include details of your beauty, unique characteristics, traits, qualities, personality, gifts, talents, appearance, and even quirks that make the special and complete package of you. Take your time—fill the space, going onto the next page—and then thank God for making you just the way He did.

Space for praising God for His *good creation*:

1 Corinthians 6:19-20, "Do you not know that your bodies are temples of the Holy Spirit, who is in you, whom you have received from God? You are not your own; you were bought at a price. Therefore honor God with your bodies."

The act of loving and appreciating ourselves as God's lovely creation means that we also respect and take care of ourselves as His creation. Instead of being self-conscious, we are going to be self-aware—aware of how to optimally take care of this body God has blessed us with. We want to bring out the best in what we've been given, by feeding our bodies nutritious food, being active, getting proper rest, and by taking the time to take care of ourselves—and not feel guilty.

Don't obsess over your looks and body image, but also don't neglect or take yourself for granted. Love and care for yourself—in this way you will honor God. Take time to nourish your body, mind, and spirit with beneficial things.

16. Now I'd like you to make a list of all the ways you plan to start loving and caring for yourself. Action steps:

The Simple Truth: You are Beautiful!

A Simple Prayer: My Dear Loving Creator, You put a lot of thought into how I was formed. Help me to appreciate the unique and special way that You made me, and to see myself through Your eyes. Beautiful. Amen.

CHAPTER SIX

You Have Purpose

The over-arching and underlying purpose of *A Daughter of the King* is to love, serve, and honor God, and in the process love, bless, and impact those around us. This greater purpose will exhibit itself differently in each of our individual lives. Words can't begin to describe the amazing joy that floods our heart as we find our purpose in God.

Proverbs 20:5, "The purposes of a person's heart are deep waters, but one who has insight draws them out."

I have heard far too many women say they aren't good at anything: they're not qualified, or useful. That's just not true. It's a lie of the enemy meant to keep us from fulfilling our God-given potential. Each of us is uniquely qualified with our talents and Spiritual gifts to do something of great purpose. It's not only what we can do, but what we can do with God working in us and through us. He is the one who calls us and equips us for the jobs, tasks, and ministries before us. If we say that we're not good at anything, we are discounting God's "good creation," and pretty much calling Him a liar. But remember who the real liar is—Satan.

Each of us is an asset in the eyes of God.

According to Merriam-Webster.com, the definition of **Asset** is *a useful or valuable thing, person, or quality*—that's YOU!

Your identity isn't what you *do*. Your identity, value, and worth are found in who you *are*—you are a child of God, and *He* has given His children the ability to do good things. Stop focusing on your weaknesses and start looking at your strengths—there you will find an outlet for your ultimate purpose.

1. What are you good at? Don't be shy; list everything that comes to mind.

2. What do you enjoy doing?

We don't need to search for some grandiose, larger-than-life expression of our purpose, we just have to look at what comes naturally—things we're good at, things we like to do, things that are on our heart, and the things and people we already have access to. It's that simple.

God doesn't use perfect people; He uses willing people.

God uses our experiences, our education—not just from the classroom—our passions, our sphere of influence, and our talents to impact the world around us.

Experiences

Your life is filled with experiences that have helped form you into the person you've become. The good, the bad, and everything in-between. God takes all of it and uses it to move you forward with purpose. I've said it before—nothing is ever wasted. Your background and experiences mold and shape your heart, your sensitivities, your goals, and they motivate your responses and actions.

Your life history can help you relate to others on a deeper level. Many ministries are started as a result of someone's personal familiarity—*been there, done that, lived through it, now let me help you*. The testimonies with the biggest impact are those that resemble your own story. Your own experiences can be used to grow compassion in you, and then be used to encourage others who are on the same journey.

Difficult *firsthand* experiences: loss, grief, divorce, abuse, addiction, etc... Satan would love for these negative hardships to hold us in bondage, away from the abundant life that God has in store for us, and also keep us from making a positive impact in the world. The enemy intends to harm us and render us ineffective by our trials, but if we let Him, God will use these for His greater purpose. Don't let Satan win by allowing him to keep his hold over you—your personal experiences can be used for good, if you surrender them to God's perfect care. Let God use your experiences to speak healing, life, encouragement, hope, and joy into the lives of others.

Romans 8:28, "And we know that in all things God works for the good of those who love him, who have been called according to his purpose."

   3. Please read the following verses regarding this truth and make note of what you learn.

- **Genesis 50:20**

- **Jeremiah 31:13**

- **2 Corinthians 1:3-4**

4. What difficult experiences can you turn over to God and allow Him to use for His greater purpose in your life, and the lives of others?

Sometimes being merely an *observer of someone else's experience* elicits a purposeful response from us, as we see their need, their pain, their poverty, or their suffering. We may be called to step into action at that very moment— we see the immediate need and meet it, right then and there. There are other times when witnessing the need of another puts a fire in our heart, stirs a passion, and develops into a longer-term mission and purpose.

Isaiah 1:17, "Learn to do right; seek justice. Defend the oppressed. Take up the cause of the fatherless; plead the case of the widow."

5. Have you ever observed someone else's experience and been prompted to act on their behalf? Describe.

Sharing life-lessons through *mentorship* is yet another way of using our experiences for the *purpose* of benefiting others. It simply means sharing the knowledge and wisdom we've gained through our own lives—our wise-ways and our mistakes—with the purpose of encouraging, teaching, and advising one another. Mentorship is leading by example, using our lives for God's purpose.

6. Please open your Bible to read what **Titus 2:3-5** has to say about mentorship. Please write out this verse and make note of your observations.

7. List some life experiences you think God wants you to share to encourage other women, and help you to strengthen your own sense of purpose in His kingdom.

Education

In our culture, the official course of education begins on the first day of kindergarten and continues through to high school graduation. Some children begin their education a year or two earlier in preschool, and others as adults, continue their education into college and graduate school. Some forego the traditional route and—like me—go onto a trade school. This has become the *general* standard, but not everyone falls into this category. Some of the wisest people I've known never made it past high school in their formal education. You see, not all education occurs within the walls of the classroom. Much of our learning occurs elsewhere—our experiences, our conversations, our observations, travel, the news, books, T.V., magazines, the internet, and most importantly, the Bible. These various forms of learning are crafted into a well-rounded education. Don't let a diploma or certificate—or lack thereof—dictate your worth or purpose. God uses it all.

Proverbs 24:3-4, "By wisdom a house is built, and through understanding it is established; ⁴ through knowledge its rooms are filled with rare and beautiful treasures."

8. Which forms of education have most impacted the way you think, live, and see the world?

Desires

Don't let insecurity stop you from pursuing the passions God has put into your heart. Refuse to listen to any voice that says, "That's a stupid idea." It was my desire—put there by God—to write this book. It's not something I'm especially qualified to do, but I followed my heart's leading. If something is pressing on your heart, I encourage you to check it out, see where it leads, and follow it through. You may be pleasantly surprised at the outcome! Your responsibility is to act in faith and obedience to whatever God places on your hearts and calls you to, and then trust Him with the results.

Psalm 37:4, "Take delight in the LORD, and he will give you the desires of your heart."

9. Name a desire/passion that is on your heart right this moment. It's time to act on it!

Sphere of influence

Home, work, school, your neighborhood, the grocery store. You have a purpose right where you are. Reach out your arms and at the end of your fingertips you will find your sphere of influence. You don't have to travel to the ends of the earth to make a difference—unless of course you are called to. You can make an impact right where you are! The people right around you need you in their life. Make yourself available, then be obedient to the LORD's promptings.

Esther 4:14, "For if you remain silent at this time, relief and deliverance for the Jews will arise from another place, but you and your father's family will perish. And who knows but that you have come to your royal position for such a time as this?"

Queen Esther began her life as an ordinary Jewish girl, but God raised her up to the position of queen, giving her access to influence the decisions of her husband, King Xerxes. As a result, she saved the Jews who were living under Persian rule, from imminent annihilation. She had a great impact in her everyday sphere of influence. You can too. You can make a difference in the lives of your family, friends, neighbors, co-workers, ministry partners, and even in the lives of complete strangers that you encounter. Look at the lives you already touch on a regular basis and there you will find your purpose.

10. Describe your current sphere of influence. Whose life do you plan on impacting positively?

Skills and Talents

Do you have a special flair, knack, or ability for certain things? Do you have a mind for numbers, a natural way with words, an ability for organization, a keen eye for décor, an aptitude for language, a talent for musical instruments, art, singing, or dancing, or are you a whiz in the kitchen? God has placed within each of us some natural abilities—certain skills and talents that come more easily—that He wants to incorporate into our purpose. Is there something you enjoy doing, anything that comes naturally for you, or something you're particularly interested in? I encourage you to think outside the box. Whatever popped in your mind, I say pursue it! There is a use for every skill and talent you have inside of you; it just might be waiting to be discovered. If you want to strengthen your ability, talents, or skill sets with some formal training I say go for it! Enroll in a class, take lessons online, expand your horizons, and foster the growth of the skills and talents that God has already bestowed on you. Have confidence in the ability He has given you! Then go on to use your God-given skills and talents to bless others.

Exodus 31:3, "and I have filled him with the Spirit of God, with wisdom, with understanding, with knowledge and with all kinds of skills…"

Just as God, in the time of Moses, gave His people the skills for building His "Tent of Meeting", God is the One who gives us the skills and abilities for the tasks He entrusts to us.

11. What comes to mind as your natural ability? What steps can you take to strengthen it?

12. How can you use your talents and skills to bless others?

Ever-changing

You never reach a point when you are no longer useful or cease to have purpose. Your purpose may evolve, but it never ends.

My over-all, and constant purpose on this earth is to love and glorify God, but beyond that God has also given me other purposes along the way. These other purposes have grown and changed over the course of my life thus far, and no doubt will continue to do so. I have devoted a large portion of my life to my marriage and to raising our two wonderful sons. I spent many years, wiping noses, reading bedtime stories, singing lullabies, watching Barney the purple dinosaur and Blues Clues, driving carpool, cheering at sporting events, all culminating with the wiping of my own tears of overwhelming pride as each of my sons walked down the aisle and received their High School diploma. Anticipating their graduation days would occasionally fill me with dread, as I wondered, "What will my purpose be now?" With them leaving the nest and living far from home, what would I do? The fear and doubt that I was losing my purpose began to creep in. I turned these thoughts over to God and He showed me that I hadn't lost my purpose, it was just changing a bit. He was right, I still have a LOT of purpose in me. Coming out of the other side of doubt, I can confidently tell you that *you never lose your purpose*.

Exodus 9:16, "But I have raised you up for this very purpose, that I might show you my power and that my name might be proclaimed in all the earth."

13. Have you ever had to let go of a purpose? Was it easy or difficult? Do you trust that God wants you to move forward, and that He has a new outlet of purpose in store for you? Are you ready to receive it?

Just as we never get too old, or outgrow having an impact, we are never too young to be used for God's greater purpose either.

1 Timothy 4:12, "Don't let anyone look down on you because you are young, but set an example for the believers in speech, in conduct, in love, in faith, and in purity."

Gifts

1 Corinthians 12:4-6, "There are different kinds of gifts, but the same Spirit distributes them. ⁵ There are different kinds of service, but the same Lord. ⁶ There are different kinds of working, but in all of them and in everyone it is the same God at work."

Each of us is born with a tendency towards certain skills and talents that can be grown and developed in us through training. Scripture tells us that we are re-born the moment we receive Jesus as our Savior, and in that very instant we are blessed with the Holy Spirit—God's Spirit—coming to dwell inside of us, sealing us as God's child. When the Holy Spirit comes to take up residence in our lives, He comes bearing gifts—Spiritual Gifts. These are gifts that we cannot earn, and ones that we cannot learn. They are given to us by the grace of God to help us fulfill our God-given purpose in the church. Everyone who knows Jesus as Savior has been blessed with Spiritual gifts—that includes *you*!

14. Please open your Bible and read all of **1 Corinthians chapter 12** to learn more about the Holy Spirit and the Spiritual gifts we receive from the LORD.

    a. What does the Holy Spirit inspire us to say about Jesus? **(verse 12:3)**

    b. In **verses 12:4-6**, the word "different" is used three times. List what it references.

c. Despite the differences, what do all gifts have in common? **(verses 12:4-6)**

d. For what reason are the gifts given? **(verse 12:7)**

e. In **verses 12:8-10**, we find a list of spiritual gifts that are distributed within the body of Christ. Please write them here.

f. Who does the distributing? **(verse 12:11)**

g. What example does Paul use to get across his point that every gift is equally important and useful in the body of Christ? Does this make it clear that no matter what gift you have, you have just as much purpose as anyone else in the body?

h. According to **1 Corinthians 13:1-13**, what is the "most excellent way" that binds all the gifts together and keeps them each functioning properly?

15. Please read the following Scriptures for some additional insight into Spiritual gifts—such as any gifts that weren't listed in 1 Corinthians 12, the reason we are given Spiritual gifts, and how we are to use them.

- **Romans 12:1-8**

- **Ephesians 4:11-16**

I love the exhortation found in **Romans 12:6-8**. It reminds me of a sporting goods commercial, as if Paul is saying, "Whatever your gift is, *just use it*! Stop worrying about what everyone else has and *use* the wonderful gifts that God has given *you*!"

Use your gift well, use it joyfully, use it in unity with others so the body of Christ can grow stronger together, and "attain to the whole measure of the fullness of Christ."

Ephesians 4:16, "From Him the whole body, joined and held together by every supporting ligament, grows and builds itself up in love, as each part does its work."

The body of Christ is meant to work together. Whether you are behind the scenes or up on stage, you are a necessary part!

You may or may not have a notion or conviction as to what gifts you have been given. Here are some clues to help you: Perhaps you are extra sensitive to the pain and hurt of others—you may have the "gift of mercy." If you often feel compelled to give to others, you just might have the "gift of giving." If you are always the first one to jump up and offer a helping hand, you quite possibly have the "gift of service." If you find that others are frequently drawn to you for godly advice, you probably have the "gift of wisdom." I'm sure you're getting the gist of it by now.

If you are uncertain at this point, there are actually tests online that can assist you in figuring out your gifting. After answering a series of questions, the survey will narrow down the results to reveal your areas of strength. After figuring out which gifts are yours, the time comes for unwrapping, appreciating, and using them. A gift that's never opened or used is, well, useless. Open your gift and let it equip you to fulfill your purpose within the church.

    16. Do you have an idea of what your gifting is yet? If so, what is it? Are you already using it?

Evolving Gifts

Finding our purpose in the church can happen quite naturally; it did for me. When my first-born was a toddler, I would drop him off each week for his Sunday school class, and each week I was given a tag with a number that corresponded with the one taped to my son's back. In case of emergencies—crying, dirty diapers, and such—they would page parents by flashing your number on the screen at the front of the sanctuary. So, each week I would drop my little guy off, and take my seat in church hoping not to see my number pop up, but week after week it did. It seems my son was experiencing a bit of separation anxiety from me, so each week I would get up from my seat and find my way to his class, where I would stay for the rest of the service. I quickly became a "helper" in the two-year-old room. This was my first foray into ministry. I then began serving alternately in the newborns room to be with my younger son as well. As my boys grew up and moved onto kindergarten, then 1st grade, 2nd grade and so on, I moved along with them. I signed up to volunteer in their classes a couple of times each month. Then I branched out and became an AWANA leader every Wednesday night. I graduated to being a head teacher for the 4/5th Saturday night service. Then for a while I helped in the Middle School room, and it was about this time that I prayed for God to show me my new purpose within the church. I prayed fervently for Him to grow me, use me and "enlarge my territory."

1 Chronicles 4:10, "Jabez cried out to the God of Israel, 'Oh, that you would bless me indeed and enlarge my territory! Let your hand be with me, and keep me from harm so that I will be free from pain.' And God granted his request."

Very soon afterward I was asked to teach a class in our church's women's ministry, where I still serve today. God has continued to grow me exponentially through the privilege of serving His women, and His church. I am doing things I would have never dreamed possible, but with the gifting, equipping, and opportunities I've received from God, I am fulfilling His purpose for me.

You see, I didn't have any special qualifications, other than being willing and ready to answer God's call— He literally called me by flashing my number across the screen.

On my own, I'm just a weak and empty vessel, but with God I am so much more! And so are you.

2 Corinthians 4:7, "But we have this treasure in jars of clay to show that this all-surpassing power is from God and not from us."

17. Have any new ministry opportunities presented themselves to you lately? Flashed across the screen for you? Pray for God's guidance.

Just because you have always been involved in one area of ministry thus far doesn't mean that is where God will have you stay plugged in forever. Be open to change, ever evolving in your service following the path that God has for you. Hold loosely to your area of service—after all, it doesn't really belong to you, it belongs to the LORD. Serving is not meant to be a burden, and it is not meant to be for your glory, but the LORD's. We are meant to experience *His joy* as we serve with Him, in *His ministry*.

Examples of Women in Ministry

1 Corinthians 15:58, "Therefore, my dear brothers and sisters, stand firm. Let nothing move you. Always give yourselves fully to the work of the Lord, because you know that your labor in the Lord is not in vain."

18. Throughout the New Testament we find examples of women who had purpose and worth and contributed greatly to the ministry of Jesus. Please read a few of their stories by opening your Bible to the Scriptures below. See if you can pin-point their part/purpose in ministry and record your findings in the space provided.

- **Lydia: Acts 16:13-15, 40**

- **Tabitha (Dorcas): Acts 9:36-43**

- **Priscilla: Acts 18:24-26**

Overlapping Skills, Talents, and Spiritual Gifts

Very often our skills, talents, and Spiritual gifts will overlap as we follow the everyday purpose that God has given us.

For example, over my life I have been a hairdresser by trade and God has used my skill to make women look pretty on the outside, but combined with my Spiritual gifts of mercy and wisdom I've also had the opportunity to make them feel beautiful on the inside. I've listened to their stories, provided a compassionate ear, and hopefully offered some godly counsel. More than once, I've had the opportunity to pray with my clients at the end of their appointments, sending them off with a bit more peace and hope than they had previously. I have purpose.

Lydia, whose story you just read in Acts 16, gives us an example of a woman who used what God had blessed her with, to in turn bless others. She was a financially successful woman—she was a dealer in expensive purple cloth—and she shared her resources with the body of Christ. Her humble gifts of service, giving, and faith, were exhibited through her generous hospitality of welcoming the body of Christ to use *her* home as *their* home-base. She had purpose.

In Acts 9, we learned that Tabitha "was always doing good and helping the poor." Her friends also said that she regularly made robes and clothes which she no doubt gave to those in need. Tabitha used her skill of sewing alongside her gifts of mercy, service, and giving to bless the community and the body of Christ. She had purpose.

As we read Priscilla's story in Acts 18, we notice that she too opened her home to a fellow brother-in-Christ, and along with her hospitality she used her "gift of teaching" to explain the complete Truth of Jesus and His Gospel message of salvation. She helped to equip Apollos for his future ministry. She had purpose.

God has blessed every one of us with special skills, talents, and gifts with which we can serve Him. There are countless unique and individual ways that God equips us. Each one of us has something special in/about us that God wants to use to bless others and bring glory to Himself, as He is the giver of all our good gifts. So, take time this week to ask God to reveal to you any talent or gift He has given and wants you to start sharing with others. It could be as simple as calling a friend who God places on your heart, because God knows you are a good listener, and He has given you the "gift of mercy."

19. Do you recognize any ways your skills, talents, and gifts can overlap in fulfilling your purpose? Describe.

Offering Hospitality is a Use of Your Purpose.

20. I'd like you to read a handful of verses on "hospitality." Even though it is not officially listed as a "gift," there is a lot we can glean about its purpose in our lives. Record what you learn through each.

- **1 Timothy 5:10**

- **Romans 12:13**

- **Hebrews 13:2**

- **1 Peter 4:9**

- **3 John 1:8**

Purpose in Everyday Life

21. **Please read Proverbs 31:10-31,** and as you do, I would like you to replace the word "wife" with the word "woman" because these *virtues* apply to women from all situations—whether you're married or have children is of no matter for our purpose here. I give you this Scripture not as an unattainable, burdensome list of all that you should be doing, but instead to show you that valuable purpose is found in our everyday living—our homes, our family, our work, our tasks, our words.

    a. Write your observations here. Which verse speaks most strongly to you?

22. Please read **Colossians 3:17** for more insight to your service. Record your findings.

Take the pressure off yourself to be perfect, and just serve when, how, and where the LORD has equipped and placed you.

Harvester

Growing up I would sometimes hear people mention the meaning of their names. Some of them had beautiful meanings that I envied. You see my full name is Tracy Ann and the meaning is *harvester- full of grace*; when I was younger, I thought it sounded bland and ordinary. Over the years I have come to greatly appreciate the beautiful and extraordinary meaning of my name.

For many years I have tried my hand at growing oranges and lemons, and each year I would get excited as the white blossoms turned into little green balls of baby fruit. These were supposed to ripen into full size fruit, but mine would inevitably all fall off to the ground below. I am happy to report that my green thumb seems to be doing much better lately. I have four fruit trees which are all doing well this season. My nectarine tree produced a large bowl of juicy, sweet fruit for me this summer. I have expanded my citrus collection to include a mandarin tree as well as the orange and lemon ones. I am very pleased to say that the little green fruits have stayed on their branches and are growing into what I hope will be an abundant harvest of healthy, yummy treats. My greatest feat this summer was harvesting an overflowing, unending supply of tomatoes and green squash. Our vigorously growing tomato plant has provided me with enough tomatoes for big bowls of fresh salsa and pots full of homemade pasta sauce. The green squash seems to be from the Jurassic period. I have never seen such huge squash in all my life, and they just keep on coming. I use them in soups, with pasta, in egg dishes, etc.

It seems that I am living up to my name and I am thoroughly enjoying it. Planting, watering, and tending to the plants is very rewarding work. The time invested is well worth it. Watching the fruit grow, bringing in the harvest, and enjoying the fruits of my labor is a wonderful blessing.

I have found though, that the best part of having the name "Harvester" is that as a child of God I am specifically called to be a *harvester*, not of fruit, but of people. God wants me and all His followers to plants seeds of love that are "full of grace," and the message of Jesus everywhere we go. It is wonderful to watch as lives are transformed, as others turn to God, and He makes *their* lives blossom into something beautiful. I am blessed to be called His harvester, and I pray that I am always full of His grace.

I have a purpose in the Kingdom of God. You have purpose in the Kingdom of God. He calls each of us to become *harvesters* for His Kingdom—planting seeds of His truth, watering with His love, and then helping to bring in the harvest of people whose hearts are searching for a place to call home. *Harvesters* welcome others into the Kingdom of God.

Matthew 9:37-38, "Then He said to his disciples, 'The harvest is plentiful but the workers are few. Ask the Lord of the harvest, therefore, to send out workers into his harvest field.'"

James 3:18, "Peacemakers who sow in peace reap a harvest of righteousness."

I pray that your heart is being tugged on with the realization that you are a blessed and beautiful *harvester* in God's Kingdom.

You are saved: Because of His love, By His power, For His purpose.

The Simple Truth: You have Purpose!

A Simple Prayer: Dear Heavenly Father, help me to appreciate the unique ways You have equipped me for Your purpose, not to envy what others do or have, but instead embrace my own calling. Show me how to best use my life to bless others and bring You glory, honor, and praise. Amen.

CHAPTER SEVEN

You are Strong

Philippians 4:13, "I can do everything through Him who gives me strength."

Insecurity is rooted in fear, and Satan loves to play on our fears: fear that we're unloved, unwanted, or undesirable; fear of rejection; fear of abandonment; fear that we're not able; fear that we're not strong enough. These fears keep us just where Satan wants us—weak, vulnerable, paralyzed, ineffective.

I have heard the term "paralyzed with fear" many times throughout my life, but it wasn't until I experienced this phenomenon firsthand that I was able to grasp just how real this statement is.

My family had taken a trip to the mountains for the weekend. It had recently been snowing and the mountain was in prime condition for some skiing and snowboarding. My husband is a very skilled skier, and our two sons are fearless snowboarders. I, on the other hand, am an eternal beginner skier. My fear of falling and the feeling of pain will keep me on the "bunny slopes" forever, and I'm ok with that. I enjoy staying on my little hill that is called "School Yard." When the kids were younger, they would stay with me on the beginner slope most of the day and then venture off for a little while for a more challenging adventure with their Dad. Nowadays they do the opposite— spending most of the day at the top of the mountain with their Dad, while checking in on me periodically throughout the day, graciously doing a run or two with dear old Mom. Well, on this particular trip my guys had persuaded me to join them on a different, slightly more advanced run, and this is when I became personally acquainted with paralyzing fear. We had made it halfway down the hill when we came to a section that to me appeared to be a sheer drop. I came to a dead stop. As my family encouraged me to keep going, I stood there literally frozen— nothing moved but my eyeballs as I scanned the scene looking for a way out. I prayed and cried, and as much as I thought about moving, I couldn't budge a muscle. At this point my husband and sons had already passed me up and couldn't do much to help, so they continued to the bottom of the mountain. A passerby tried to help me, but I think my near hysteria scared him away. The next thing I knew my husband appeared by my side. He had gone to the bottom of the slope, gotten back on the chairlift, which brought him back up the mountain so he could ski down to the place where I was at. My big, strong husband had come to rescue me and guide me to safety. He helped me to get back up (by this time I was sitting on the hill) and then he had me stand behind him with my skis placed between his own. He planned to ski me down the mountain. He told me to hold on and keep my skis lined up straight with his. My husband is 6'5" and standing behind him I couldn't see a thing ahead of me. I also had no control of where I was going. I simply trusted him to get me safely down the hill. I remember wrapping my arms around his waist and the smell of his freshly laundered clothing. I remember the great relief I felt as I watched the scenery whizzing by out of the corner of my eye. I remember thinking that he was my hero. I had bravely made it down the mountain and it wasn't because I had faith in my own ability. I was brave because I had faith in my husband's ability and the love he has for me.

As much as my husband was my hero that day, God is my true Hero every day. My paralyzing fears are conquered as I trust Him to safely deliver me in, through, and out of every situation I may encounter. God's ability and love for me puts all my fears to rest. God says "Grab hold of me, I've got you. In Me you will find bravery and strength."

Psalm 63:8, "I cling to you; your right hand upholds me."

God is Strong

1. We are brave because of the One in whom our faith is placed. Please read the following verses and make note on what each one reveals about the strength of God.

- **Deuteronomy 3:21-24**

- **Isaiah 40:25-26**

- **Zephaniah 3:17**

God is Faithful

2. Our faith is built on Someone who is faithful. Please read the following Scriptures to learn more about the faithfulness of God. Make notes on each reference.

- **Deuteronomy 7:9**

- **Psalm 36:5**

- **Isaiah 25:1**

- **2 Timothy 2:13**

Strong in the LORD

When life gets tough, we often try to muster the strength to get ourselves through a situation, but we quickly become tired under the weight of it all. Sometimes we turn to others for strength, looking for their boost of muscle to carry us through—this is good in the short-term, but they too will eventually grow weak. Jesus is the One with the strong arms we need to carry us through; His strength never falters, never weakens, and never fails.

We are only as strong as the One we place our faith in.

3. Please look up the following verses and make note of your observations.

- **Psalm 27:14**

- **Psalm 31:24**

- **Psalm 73:26**

- Psalm 68:35

Throughout the pages of Scripture, we find stories of ordinary individuals—just like you and me—who did extraordinary things because of the God who strengthened them. David, a mere shepherd boy, struck down the feared giant Goliath with one stone. God's power was at work in him. Moses, at one time insecure and frightened, became a determined and confident individual who led the nation of Israel to freedom and the Promised Land. God's power was at work in him. Paul, a faithful servant of the LORD, was beaten, imprisoned, mocked, shipwrecked, flogged, starved, and left for dead, yet he joyfully proclaimed the Good News of Jesus till his last day on earth and his teachings are impacting millions to this day. God's power was at work in him. God strengthened each of these individuals through some enormous obstacles and He can strengthen you too.

Deuteronomy 31:6, "Be strong and courageous. Do not be afraid or terrified because of them, for the LORD your God goes with you; he will never leave you nor forsake you."

God's Great Power

Ephesians 1:15-23, "For this reason, ever since I heard about your faith in the Lord Jesus and your love for all God's people, **¹⁶** I have not stopped giving thanks for you, remembering you in my prayers. **¹⁷** I keep asking that the God of our Lord Jesus Christ, the glorious Father, may give you the Spirit of wisdom and revelation, so that you may know him better. **¹⁸** I pray that the eyes of your heart may be enlightened in order that you may know the hope to which he has called you, the riches of his glorious inheritance in his holy people, **¹⁹** and his incomparably great power for us who believe. That power is the same as the mighty strength **²⁰** he exerted when he raised Christ from the dead and seated him at his right hand in the heavenly realms, **²¹** far above all rule and authority, power and dominion, and every name that is invoked, not only in the present age but also in the one to come. **²²** And God placed all things under his feet and appointed him to be head over everything for the church, **²³** which is his body, the fullness of him who fills everything in every way."

    4.   Regarding **Ephesians 1:15-23** please answer the following questions.

   a.   What words are used to describe God's power?

   b.   What authority does the power of Christ have? What is it over and above?

   c.   How was God's power exhibited in Christ?

d. For whom else is this power at work?

e. What are the blessings of His power in us?

These Scriptures should encourage us beyond belief! The same incredible power that brought Jesus back from the dead and placed Him—alive, well, and glorified—in authority over everything in heaven and earth, is working for us! This power enlightens us to understand and know the LORD better; it enables us to experience the hope of our eternal standing now and forever!

To know the power of God is an amazing thing!

For Us, In Us, Through Us

We are strong not because of what *we* can do, we are strong because of what *God* can do for us, in us, and through us!

2 Corinthians 12:9-10, "⁹ But he said to me, 'My grace is sufficient for you, for my power is made perfect in weakness.' Therefore I will boast all the more gladly about my weaknesses, so that Christ's power may rest on me. ¹⁰ That is why, for Christ's sake, I delight in weaknesses, in insults, in hardships, in persecutions, in difficulties. For when I am weak, then I am strong."

- **For us**: His power saved us from sin, eternal death, and condemnation. His power brought us forgiveness, eternal life, and freedom.
- **In us**: His power renews, invigorates, refreshes, and strengthens us. His power gives us a new perspective, a fresh hope, a bold confidence. His power changes us from the inside out.
- **Through us**: His power equips us to impact family, friends and the world around us.

In the strength of Jesus and through the power of the Holy Spirit we can:

- Overcome sin
- Forgive others
- Forgive ourselves
- Stand strong in our convictions
- Face persecution
- Persevere triumphantly

- Endure pain and suffering
- Resist temptation
- Love difficult people
- Hold our tongue
- Conquer fear
- Calm anxiety
- Step out of depression
- Change our negative thinking
- Break free from addiction
- Transform a bad attitude
- Let go of bitterness
- Experience healing
- Obey the LORD
- Stand victorious
- Etc.

His power provides all we need for daily living.

The more we seek, know, and believe God—take Him at His Word—and allow His Spirit to grab hold of us, the more His strength is able to build us up and equip us for the journey.

2 Peter 1:3, "His divine power has given us everything we need for a godly life through our knowledge of him who called us by his own glory and goodness."

5. How can God's strength and power help us with each of the items listed above?

6. Which phrase from the list stands out as the area you most need the power of God right now? Feel free to make up your own.

7. In which areas have you already been helped by the power of God?

Ephesians 3:20-21, "Now to him who is able to do immeasurably more than all we ask or imagine, according to his power that is at work within us, ²¹ to him be glory in the church and in Christ Jesus throughout all generations, for ever and ever! Amen."

The Battle Belongs to the LORD

There is a war that is raging all around us. It is an unseen war, a spiritual war. Satan is the instigator, initiator, and evil, rebellious force behind this war. In his awful pride he has pitted himself against God Almighty, Jesus Christ, and all of Jesus' followers. Satan's whole purpose is to keep people from accepting Jesus Christ as their Savior and receiving eternal life. If you have accepted Christ, then you have already won the war and are safe and secure in the hands of God for all of eternity. Although we are on the winning side, we will still endure attacks. We have a choice as to the part we will play in the ongoing battles: the helpless victim, or the powerful warrior that we truly are in Christ. Attacks will come in various ways—physical, spiritual, emotional, mental. Satan knows our eternal fate is secure, but he wants to disrupt and destroy our daily life by making us feel defeated. He wants us to feel anything but strong. He desperately wants to steer our focus off God and steal the glorious abundant life that is rightfully ours in Christ.

God always wins and the war with Satan is no exception. We are on the winning side. Let that Truth sink in and fill you with confidence.

Deuteronomy 28:7, "The LORD will grant that the enemies who rise up against you will be defeated before you. They will come at you from one direction but flee from you in seven."

8. Please read the following verses describing the battle and make note of your observations.

- **Psalm 140:7**

- **1 Peter 5:8-9**

- **John 10:10**

- John 16:33

- James 4:7

- 2 Thessalonians 3:3

- 1 Corinthians 4:20

The Armor of God

Ephesians 6:10-18, "Finally, be strong in the Lord and in his mighty power. [11] Put on the full armor of God, so that you can take your stand against the devil's schemes. [12] For our struggle is not against flesh and blood, but against the rulers, against the authorities, against the powers of this dark world and against the spiritual forces of evil in the heavenly realms. Therefore, put on the full armor of God, so that when the day of evil comes, you may be able to stand your ground, and after you have done everything, to stand. [14] Stand firm then, with the belt of truth buckled around your waist, with the breastplate of righteousness in place, [15] and with your feet fitted with the readiness that comes from the gospel of peace. [16] In addition to all this, take up the shield of faith, with which you can extinguish all the flaming arrows of the evil one. [17] Take the helmet of salvation and the sword of the Spirit, which is the word of God. [18] And pray in the Spirit on all occasions with all kinds of prayers and requests. With this in mind, be alert and always keep on praying for all the Lord's people."

9. According to **Ephesians 6:10-18**, we learn that God has equipped us with His spiritual armor enabling us to stand victorious in our daily battles against the enemy. Please answer the related questions.

    a. List the pieces of Armor and write your understanding of each.

More space for listing:

b. Whose Armor are we using?

c. How does His Armor help us?

d. What action words are used to describe our part in using the Armor?

e. Why do you suppose the "Belt of Truth" is the first item put on?

f. According to **verse 6:18** what is the additional, yet vitally important component that we are encouraged to use in our battle?

Let's take a closer look at our armor. Each individual piece has a unique function, yet it overlaps and interlinks with all the others.

The Belt of Truth

Truth marks us as God's child, different from the world. Putting on the Belt of Truth means that our life is built and based on what God says about anything and everything. God's truth is unchanging, unwavering, solid, and eternal. His Truth brings stability to our lives since it isn't based on our ever-changing emotions, feelings, desires, perspective, or on what society says is truth. His Truth is objective, holy, pure, good, and perfect. Putting on the Belt of Truth means anchoring our life to God's perspective and standard, and judging all else accordingly. The enemy would love to get us off track from the Truth—he is always ready to feed us a lie. If you are ever uncertain of what Truth really is, just open your Bible for a good reminder. The Belt of Truth is the first item we put on, and the Truth to which all the other pieces are anchored.

John 14:6, "Jesus answered, 'I am the way and the truth and the life. No one comes to the Father except through me.'"

    10. What lies have you been believing?

    11. Do you need to adjust your perspective to match that of God's Truth? How do you plan on doing this?

The Breastplate of Righteousness

Righteousness is the practical application of Truth in our lives—living out our new identity in Christ with purity and righteousness, aligning our lives to God's holiness. Unchecked sin is like holes in our armor—a place left undefended, open, and vulnerable. Sin is an open invitation for the enemy to attack. Right living seals up our armor, rendering it impenetrable, removing opportunities for regret, shame, condemnation.

Leviticus 19:2, "Therefore, be holy, as I am holy."

    12. What unchecked holes in your armor (sin) need to be dealt with?

    13. What action steps can you take to seal up those holes?

Shoes of the Gospel of Peace

Through the death, burial, and resurrection of Jesus Christ we have peace with God—that is the Gospel (the Good News) in a nutshell. The obstacles of sin, death, and condemnation are removed from us forever. We have a direct line of communication with our Heavenly Father. Jesus has removed the enmity and hostility which previously kept us from Him—we have *peace with God*. Through Jesus Christ we also have been bestowed with the additional blessing of the peace *of* God. You may be asking what the difference is in this minute variation of wording. Well, simply put, the *peace of God* is the peace that surpasses all human understanding. It is a settled assurance within our soul that everything is going to be OK, despite our current circumstances. Satan loves nothing more than to get us all worked up and bring turmoil into our hearts and minds, but with the *peace of God* we are equipped to remain steady and unshaken by the events and issues that are attacking us. Our peace *with* God and *of* God equips us to go out and *share His message of peace with the chaotic world around us.*

Philippians 4:7, "And the peace of God, which transcends all understanding, will guard your hearts and your minds in Christ Jesus."

14. Have you made peace *with* God through His Son, Jesus Christ?

15. How can you take advantage of the peace *of* God in your life daily?

16. With whom can you share the message of God's peace?

Shield of Faith

Faith is *believing and acting* on God's Truth (hence the saying, "step out in faith.") It is trusting in God's ability and His Word. Faith is believing what God says over what we can see—it is seeing the possible, in the impossible. A mindset of faith leaves no room for worry or fear. A mindset of faith must be purposefully and continually chosen. Faith is claiming that if God says it, then it must be true. Lack of faith is the biggest hindrance to the abundant life God has for each of us—that's why Satan constantly whispers notions of doubt. The shield of faith extinguishes all the flaming arrows of doubt that the enemy shoots at us.

Psalm 84:11-12, "For the LORD God is a sun and shield, the LORD bestows favor and honor; no good thing does he withhold from those whose walk is blameless. ¹² LORD Almighty, blessed is the one who trusts in you."

17. Is lack of faith hindering your walk with the LORD? Is it keeping you from the abundant life He has in store for you? If you feel you're lacking in the faith department, I want you to know there is no shame in asking God to increase your belief in Him, and for the courage to step out. There is in fact a precedence for this request found in **Mark 9:24**, which I'm encouraging you to read.

Helmet of Salvation

Salvation represents who we are in Christ—saved and redeemed, fresh and new, set free, a child of God. The helmet of Salvation protects our mind from the lies regarding our identity that try to infiltrate and destroy. Satan greatly desires that we forget who we really are, and all the benefits that have been given to us. If we forget we are *a daughter of the King*, and that we have access to the heavenly resources of God, then Satan is definitely at an advantage over us. Salvation is not only what we are saved *from* (the wrath and judgment of God), but also what we are saved *to*—free and abundant life here on earth, glorious eternal life in Heaven.

Galatians 5:1, "It is for freedom that Christ has set us free. Stand firm, then, and do not let yourselves be burdened again by a yoke of slavery."

18. What lies have you been believing regarding your identity?

19. How is God's Word changing that belief?

20. Do you believe that God came to set you free from the bondage of self-doubt?

Sword of the Spirit (the Word of God)

The Sword of the Spirit is both a defensive and offensive weapon that is ours to confidently wield, in fighting back any attacks and lies from the enemy. Any time he speaks untruths to us we are to immediately *turn our thoughts to the encouragements that God has spoken personally to us through His Word*—the ones that have popped off the page at us, the ones that were spoken in a church service that we know were meant just for us, the ones that we've tucked securely into our hearts. The Word of God has power in our lives—power to save us, change us, comfort us, encourage us, teach us, admonish us, lead us, and the power to refute the lies of the enemy. God's Word is living and active.

Hebrews 4:12, "For the word of God is alive and active. Sharper than any double-edged sword, it penetrates even to dividing soul and spirit, joints and marrow; it judges the thoughts and attitudes of the heart."

21. Do you have any favorite verses that bring you comfort and courage in the battles of everyday life? If so, write them here. If not, dig into your Bible and ask God to reveal a treasure from His Word directly to your heart. You can also look back over this study and gather the verses that most spoke to your heart, and compile them on a page, or in a journal for easy reference in the future.

2 Corinthians 10:4-5, "The weapons we fight with are not the weapons of the world. On the contrary, they have divine power to demolish strongholds. ⁵ We demolish arguments and every pretension that sets itself up against the knowledge of God, and we take captive every thought to make it obedient to Christ."

The Armor of God is simply your identity in Christ. Stand firm in who God is and in who you are—you are loved, you are forgiven and new, you belong, you matter, you are beautiful, you have purpose, you are strong, and you are royalty. You are a daughter of the King; you are a child of God.

Ephesians 6:10, "Finally, be strong in the Lord and in his mighty power."

His Strength is Ours

When I was a young girl, my Grandma taught me this amazing truth: as a child of God I am in the privileged position to call on the name and power of Jesus to defend me, and I am also in the position to stand in confident authority against Satan and his schemes.

22. Please read the following verses and make note of the encouragements.

- **2 Timothy 1:7**

- **1 John 2:14**

- 1 John 4:4

- Revelation 12:11

Strength in Our Identity

Ephesians 3:16-18, "I pray that out of his glorious riches he may strengthen you with power through his Spirit in your inner being, so that Christ may dwell in your hearts through faith. And I pray that you, being rooted and established in love. ^{18} may have power, together with all the Lord's holy people, to grasp how wide and long and high and deep is the love of Christ, ^{19} and to know this love that surpasses knowledge—that you may be filled to the measure of all the fullness of God."

Let the love and power of Christ fill your inner being—refreshing the very depths of your soul.

A defeatist attitude will always bring defeat. You are capable of exhibiting strength beyond measure as you *choose* to put on love, faith, hope, and joy. *Choose daily to be an overcomer with the power and strength of Jesus at work in you!*

Psalm 73:26, "My flesh and my heart may fail, but God is the strength of my heart and my portion forever."

Love

The love of God makes us conquerors in more ways than we can even count—His love saves, His love lives, His love guides and admonishes, His love refreshes and comforts, His love protects, His love strengthens... Whenever we feel weak or powerless, we need only reflect on the sacrificial love that the Father has lavished on us.

Romans 8:37, "We are more than conquerors through Him who loved us."

23. How are you being strengthened by the love of God?

Faith

Faith is trusting God, inviting Him to work. Faith is our doorway to the power of God.

Matthew 17:20, "Truly I tell you, if you have faith as small as a mustard seed, you can say to this mountain, 'Move from here to there,' and it will move. Nothing will be impossible for you."

Scripture tells us that all things are possible with God—with faith of the tiniest amount, even as small as a mustard seed, we can move mountains. The seemingly insurmountable obstacles that stand in our way of living the abundant life God has in store for us— the valleys of depression, and the chains of fear that hold us captive—can all be overcome as we surrender to *God*, rely on *God*, walk in obedience to *God*, and invite the power of *God* to move in our lives. When in doubt refocus on God.

24. What mountains in your life need to be moved? Are you focused on God or the situation looming before you? Remember who your God is and be filled with fearless faith.

Hope

Isaiah 40:31, "but those who hope in the LORD will renew their strength. They will soar on wings like eagles; they will run and not grow weary, they will walk and not be faint."

The key to not being defeated is keeping your mind and heart set on *hope*. You have been given promises of great hope—you are saved, you are redeemed, you have the Holy Spirit to guide and comfort you, you have the hope of heaven for all of eternity, you have Jesus with you every moment, you have hope in knowing that your trials on earth are a tiny blip in the timeline of eternity. Hope, my dear friend, is recognizing Jesus in the moment and clinging to Him for strength, while still holding onto hope that with Jesus there is always something better on the horizon. Hope restores life. Hope is the tender voice of God calling us onward.

25. Please read **Romans 5:1-5** and **Proverbs 13:12** and make note of what your trials accomplish in you, and also what you learn about *hope*.

Joy

Nehemiah 8:10, "Do not grieve, for the joy of the LORD is your strength."

No matter how I'm feeling on a given day, joy is the fuel which refreshes my soul. I can wake up with aches and pain and still step out of bed with a song in my heart. Actually, it's a verse—albeit some days I do have to purposefully choose this mindset. Choosing a joyful mindset, counting our blessings, giving praise and thanksgiving to the LORD are all ways to restore our joy. And where does strength come from? JOY.

26. Please read **Psalm 118:24** to see what verse pops into my head. How can you start choosing joy for your own strength?

The Spirit

We do not win any battle on our own. Only as God's Spirit and His Truth go to work in our lives are we able to become more than conquerors. His Spirit commands the waves and the wind. His Spirit breathes life into us our weary bodies when we feel like giving up.

Zechariah 4:6, "'Not by might nor by power, but by my Spirit,' says the LORD Almighty."

27. Do you need the fresh wind of God's Spirit to revive you right now? If so, ask Him for a fresh filling.

If you feel the inclination to go deeper in your understanding of the Spirit you can read the additional verses of **Acts 1:8,** and **John 14:26**. Space for notes:

Be Strong, Be Still

Our LORD God Almighty gives us every reason for confidence. He is mighty and powerful, loving and good. He is fully aware of everything we battle daily, and He isn't just *with us*, He fights *for us*. We need only remember that He is our capable Father, and we are His beloved child, then stand back in awe and witness His power as He moves in our life. Sometimes it takes great strength to restrain ourselves from taking everything into our own hands. Sometimes God asks us to simply wait on Him, trust Him and watch Him move. He is mighty to save even without our effort. There can be amazing strength found in our stillness.

Exodus 14:14, "The LORD will fight for you; you need only to be still."

28. How easy is it for you to hand complete control over to God? Do you trust Him as your Defender? Explain.

Inviting God's Power through Prayer

Mighty things happen when we invite God into the situation.

29. Please read the following verses for a view of God's mighty power on behalf of those who ask (pray) and believe. Make note of what these verses mean to you.

- **Luke 11:9-13**

- **Acts 4:31**

- **Acts 16:22-26**

Did you notice that our prayers open the door to the heart and power of the Lord? We pray, He empowers us to testify on His behalf. We pray, He makes us bold. We pray, He fills us with hope. We pray, He sets us free from the chains that hold us in captivity, and He releases us from everything that imprisons us. We pray, He fills us with peace and joy. His power is readily available to us. We need only ask.

Luke 11:10, "For everyone who asks receives; the one who seeks finds; and to the one who knocks, the door will be opened."

Wave Princess

One summer day my aunt and I ventured to the beach for an outing. I had brought along my bodyboard in hopes of catching a few waves. I know this sport is often reserved for the younger crowd, but maybe I fit the bill since I like to consider myself young at heart. My board is pinkish purple in color and is called "Wave Princess." I sat on the shore with my aunt for a while, warming my body in the bright sunshine, also building the courage to enter the brisk water rolling in before me. Eventually, I left the comfort of my chair and the safety of the sand, and with my board tucked under my arm I made my way to the waters' edge. First, I dipped my toes in, then I waded deeper into the water, until finally the chilly waves splashed completely over me. I let out a shriek as the cool water shocked me for a brief second, taking my breath away; soon though the temperature felt perfect for such a warm day, refreshing and heavenly.

As I stood there facing the approaching waves a beautiful song came to mind—the lyrics spoke of how the love of God inspires bravery in us, and of how He calls us to step from the safety of the shore and out into the sometimes-tumultuous waves of life, with Him by our side. At that moment, I was comforted by the realization that whatever God calls me to— whatever opportunity, situation, blessing or problem, relationship, or task— He is always with me, He's beside me and will never leave me. That makes me brave, even willing to face the seemingly impossible. With God as my strength, no wave will ever overtake me. He makes me brave enough to get out of my comfy chair and strong enough to step beyond the shore into the tumbling waves. He makes me feel like a *Wave Princess*. I hope that my illustration encourages you to step bravely out into the waves of life as you remember that you are a Princess as well.

Hebrews 13:5-6, "for He Himself has said, 'I will never desert you, nor will I ever forsake you,' ⁶ so that we confidently say, 'The LORD is my helper, I will not be afraid.'"

God is with you. His Spirit is in you. He is your Helper. By His power you are strong, you are powerful, you are an overcomer.

The Simple Truth: You are Strong!

A Simple Prayer: Dear Almighty God, my strength is found in You alone. I am so grateful for Your love and power, which are at work in my life. You are mighty to save. Help me to keep focused on You. Amen.

CHAPTER EIGHT

Have you ever been out and about and encountered a princess in your midst? Have you ever been at the market only to look down and see one standing in line in front of you? Have you ever seen one running, climbing, and jumping at the neighborhood park in her lovely gown? There have been many times that I've come across a little girl who is dressed up in her princess gown, sparkly shoes, and even a tiara. While going about the course of my ordinary day, I cross paths with a little girl who feels extraordinary in her identity as a princess.

There is a deep desire in each woman's heart to be a princess. Even you if prefer wearing pants over frilly dresses, there is something within you that longs to be cherished, thought of as precious, and worth pursuing. There are many movies that play out the storyline of a young maiden longing for something better, a home in the royal palace, life in an enchanted far-away kingdom, with the security, safety, and love of her prince continually surrounding her. These tales resonate within our hearts. As much as this theme is viewed as pure fantasy, let me assure you, it is very real. Jesus is our Prince and our King. He has a royal home for us, which is in His Royal Kingdom, where we will live with Him for all eternity. I have compiled many Scriptures to teach us and reassure us of these truths. So, let's get started with two verses describing Jesus' royal position.

Isaiah 9:6, "For to us a child is born, to us a son is given, and the government will be on his shoulders. And he will be called Wonderful Counselor, Mighty God, Everlasting Father, Prince of Peace."

Revelation 17:14, "They will wage war against the Lamb, but the Lamb will triumph over them because he is Lord of lords and King of kings—and with him will be his called, chosen and faithful followers."

Jesus, our Prince, our King is perfect in every way. He is holy, righteous, and just; He is loving, kind, gracious, and merciful. He is sovereign overall. Nothing escapes His notice, no one escapes His care. He is the One we have been waiting for.

God's Kingdom

A perfect King undoubtedly rules a perfect Kingdom.

1. Please read the following verses detailing God's Kingdom and record the specifics of what you learn about His Kingdom beside each reference.

- **Psalm 145:13**

- **Romans 14:17**

- **2 Timothy 4:18**

- **Hebrews 1:8**

- **Hebrews 12:28-29**

- **2 Peter 1:11**

God's Kingdom is described as an everlasting, eternal, heavenly Kingdom, in authority over every other kingdom of this earth; it is a place of safety, ruled with God's perfect justice, filled with an atmosphere of righteousness, peace and joy. And being familiar with California earthquakes, I love the idea of living in a kingdom that can't ever be shaken but will remain firm forever. God's Kingdom sounds perfect to me.

Inheriting the Kingdom

The Kingdom of God flips many earthly philosophies on their head. Whereas the world sees the attributes listed in **Matthew 5:1-12** as negative weaknesses, to be avoided at all costs, God views them as positive strengths, and opportunities for His blessing. Jesus promises reward for all God's children. Please open your Bible and read through the beautiful verses in **Matthew 5:1-12**.

2. Please read through the verses listed below once more. As you do, circle the attribute that God desires in each of us, and underline the corresponding blessing and reason we can *rejoice and be glad*. Next to each write your short interpretation of what they mean.

Matthew 5: 1-12, "Now when Jesus saw the crowds, he went up on a mountainside and sat down. His disciples came to him, ² and he began to teach them.

He said:

³ 'Blessed are the poor in spirit,
   for theirs is the kingdom of heaven.

⁴ Blessed are those who mourn,
   for they will be comforted.

⁵ Blessed are the meek,
   for they will inherit the earth.

⁶ Blessed are those who hunger and thirst for righteousness,
   for they will be filled.

⁷ Blessed are the merciful,
   for they will be shown mercy.

⁸ Blessed are the pure in heart,
   for they will see God.

⁹ Blessed are the peacemakers,
   for they will be called children of God.

¹⁰ Blessed are those who are persecuted because of righteousness,
   for theirs is the kingdom of heaven.

¹¹ "Blessed are you when people insult you, persecute you and falsely say all kinds of evil against you because of me. ¹² Rejoice and be glad, because great is your reward in heaven, for in the same way they persecuted the prophets who were before you.'"

Let's take a more in-depth look at each of the verses, as we go over them one-by-one and uncover their meaning together. Keep in mind: *Blessed* means to be happy and joyful in Jesus!

"Blessed are the poor in spirit, for theirs is the kingdom of heaven."

Our entrance into the Kingdom of Heaven is found in Jesus Christ alone. It is not earned through our own efforts or capabilities, not by our achievements or merit. It is only possible as we *recognize our own spiritual deficits and see our desperate need for the Savior*—that is what it really means to be "poor in spirit." Being "poor in spirit" is the key to unlocking abundant blessings and causes the doors of Heaven to swing wide open for us. Please read the following verses regarding a *poor spirit* and make notes on each.

- **Psalm 51:17**

- **Isaiah 66:2**

3. How has your understanding of being "poor in spirit" changed because of these verses?

"Blessed are those who mourn, for they will be comforted."

When we come to Christ our sins suddenly stand out in sharp contrast to His perfect holiness, causing us to mourn what we see in ourselves. Having placed our faith in Jesus for our salvation and our way into the Kingdom, we become all too aware of our sinful nature. The ugliness of our sin brings sorrow, which leads us to repentance, which then leads us to the comforting grace, mercy, and forgiveness of our loving Father.

4. Please read the following verses which speak of mourning, repentance, and comfort. Make notes regarding each.

- **Isaiah 49:13**

- **2 Corinthians 7:10**

- **James 4:8-10**

5. Describe how *mourning* your sin is an opportunity for God to comfort you.

"Blessed are the meek (gentle, humble), for they will inherit the earth."

Don't confuse meekness with weakness. When Jesus walked this earth, He perfectly exemplified meekness for us. He is powerful and mighty, yet is described as gentle and humble. He exhibited this balanced blend of attributes as He surrendered Himself to the Father's plan, sacrificing His life for ours. So, with Jesus as our example, what does meekness look like in own lives? It simply means that we also humbly surrender ourselves to the Fathers' plan by seeking Him, and His ways for our lives. We can surrender in confidence because we know who God is, and who we are in Him. Being a child of God means we are humble in ourselves, while being confident in God and in our grace-given identity as His daughter. We will inherit the earth.

6. Look up the following verses for more insight into *meekness*. Record your observations beside each.

- **Psalm 25:9**

- **Philippians 2:5-11**

- **James 4:10**

7. What does this perfect blend of humility and confidence look like in your life?

"Blessed are those who hunger and thirst for righteousness, for they will be filled."

Jesus is the only righteous One—the only One truly approved in God's eyes—to ever walk this earth. Scripture says our righteousness is like dirty rags before the LORD (Isaiah 64:6). We could never clean ourselves up enough to be deemed right in God's eyes. Fortunately, because of Jesus' sacrifice and our faith in Him, God sees us through the covering of Jesus' righteousness. Since God now sees us this way, our heart's desire is to actively pursue righteousness—that which is acceptable to God—in our daily lives. We yearn to become more and more like our Savior. We long to please God and live a life that represents Him well. We thirst for His righteousness to reign in our mind, heart, and body. He is faithful to fill us.

8. Please check out the following verses on *righteousness* and make note of your findings.

- **Romans 6:18-23**

- **Philippians 3:7-11**

9. Is it your heart's desire to become more like Jesus? Keep seeking after Him; He will fill that desire.

"Blessed are the merciful, for they will be shown mercy."

We have come to what may be the most difficult of the Beatitudes to which we must surrender. The preceding verses relate to the relationship between us and God, while this one focuses on the relationship between us and others. Being merciful may be hard sometimes, but as we follow through out of obedience, the blessings from God will surely follow. A heart full of mercy is freed of bitterness.

10. Please read the following verses for more insight on *mercy*.

- **Luke 6:35-36**

- **Matthew 5:43-48**

11. Recognizing the undeserved *mercy* that God has bestowed on us should make it much easier to show mercy to other undeserving people. As we extend forgiveness to others, we are expressing our appreciation and gratitude for the compassion God has generously shown us. Has your heart been transformed by God's mercy, better enabling you to give grace and mercy to others?

"Blessed are the pure in heart, for they will see God."

To truly see God means to perceive, discern, be aware of Him, and to experience Him fully with our heart and mind. To truly see Him, our hearts must be free of all contaminants; they have to be pure. Our searching, our longing, our living, our serving must all spring from a pure motive of knowing God more. A pure heart has been perfectly cleansed and is continually kept clean from potential impurities. In a pure heart, everything is run through the filter of God's love—everything that comes into our hearts and everything that goes out. Much that comes in can obscure our vision of God: things such as bitterness, hatred, anger, fear, worry, anxiety, pride, etc. However, when we allow His love to clean and filter out such rubbish, and set our heart fully on Him, it is then that we will see Him clearly.

12. Read the following verses for more insight on a *pure heart*.

- **Psalm 15:1-5**

- **Psalm 24:3-6**

- **Psalm 51:10**

13. What do you need to filter out of your heart so you can see God more clearly? What can you do to make sure your vision of God is clear?

"Blessed are the peacemakers, for they will be called children of God."

God our Father is the ultimate Peacemaker. He sent His Son to restore peace between Himself and us. We are God's children, and thus carry a family resemblance. And in the footsteps of our Father, we will carry on the family heritage of being peacemakers. As children of God, we are meant to build bridges, not walls. Bringing peace to this world as representatives of Jesus means we must let go of getting our own way, and instead are always seeking Jesus' way in every matter.

14. Check out the following verses for more insight into *peacemaking*.

- **Psalm 34:14**

- **Romans 12:17-21**

15. What are some ways you can bring peace to those around you?

"Blessed are those who are persecuted because of righteousness, for theirs is the kingdom of heaven.[11] **"Blessed are you when people insult you, persecute you and falsely say all kinds of evil against you because of me.** [12] **Rejoice and be glad, because great is your reward in heaven, for in the same way they persecuted the prophets who were before you."**

These verses stand in direct opposition to our natural feelings. Normally we would run the other way when faced with persecution and insults. Jesus gave us these words as encouragement. He has warned us that just as He faced adversaries, as His followers we will too. Not everyone we encounter will feel the way we do about Jesus, and they will let us know it. But we don't have to be afraid or let them deflate our confidence, because we have an amazing, victorious award awaiting us in Heaven. All the persecution and insults we could possibly face here will fade from memory when we stand in the glory of Heaven. So, persevere during your time here on earth, as you cling to the promise of Heaven.

16. Please read the following Scriptures and record what you learn about the persecution we may face as followers of Jesus.

- **John 15:18-21**

- **Philippians 1:27-30**

17. How does the promise of Heaven equip you with confidence to face anything that comes at you?

1 John 3:1-3, "See what great love the Father has lavished on us, that we should be called children of God! And that is what we are! The reason the world does not know us is that it did not know him. ² Dear friends, now we are children of God, and what we will be has not yet been made known. But we know that when Christ appears, we shall be like him, for we shall see him as he is. ³ All who have this hope in him purify themselves, just as he is pure."

The Kingdom of God comprises of citizens who love the Lord with all their heart, soul, and mind. Its citizens are those who have recognized their need for a Savior, are repentant of their sin, seek lives of righteousness and peace, and are full of humility. What an awesome blessing we have to look forward to—sharing a heavenly Kingdom with fellow citizens who share such a lovely mindset.

Heir and Inheritance

Not only are you a citizen in the Kingdom of Heaven, but Scripture says you are also an heir, and the Kingdom is your inheritance. You don't just get the privilege of living there, it belongs to you. As God's child, you have a share in the Kingdom. The value of the eternal inheritance you will receive from your heavenly Father far outweighs any earthly inheritance you could receive from your earthly family.

Romans 8:17, "Now if we are children, then we are heirs—heirs of God and co-heirs with Christ, if indeed we share in his sufferings in order that we may also share in his glory."

18. Please read the next collection of Scriptures for further confirmation of this truth. Make note of what you learn about your position as heir and your inheritance.
    - **Galatians 4:7**

    - **Palm 37:18**

    - **Colossians 1:12-14**

    - **1 Peter 1:3-9**

Royal Home

Home. What a beautiful word! It represents a place where we belong and matter; a place where love and warmth abound. For me "home" brings memories of my Grandma and Grandpa's house. Their home will always hold a place of important significance in my heart, not because it was big or fancy, but because of the two people who lived there and the unconditional way they welcomed me. My Grandma and Grandpa (Tata) were two of the most genuine, loving, giving people I've ever met. Growing up I spent most weekends at my grandparents' home. Some of my most simple, yet special memories were made there.

Grandma and I would make chocolate chips cookies every time I stayed over. She always made sure to have the ingredients on hand—I still know the recipe by heart. Grandma had a special, teal-colored stool that she sat on at the kitchen counter all the time. Tata would take his seat at the end of the kitchen table. They drank Folgers instant coffee. My drawings hung scotch-taped onto the kitchen walls. I ate quesadillas, frozen pizzas, and frozen chicken T.V. dinners there (I was a child of the 70's). Tata would pull Abazaba candy bars out of my ears and pull me around the floor on a blanket. Grandma would rub Vick's VapoRub on my chest when I was sick. I would spend hours playing with my dolls on the living room floor. Grandma taught me how to play Solitaire, and we would play Go Fish and Tiddly Winks together. I watched The Love Boat at night (I'm not sure how appropriate that was), and morning cartoons when I woke up. This is where I learned to look up in the sky and witness God's handiwork as we searched for the Big and Little Dippers together. When I was little Grandma would rock me to sleep on her lap as she sang "Hush Little Baby", and the chair we were sitting on would creak in rhythm as she rocked back and forth. She prepared a bed in the back room especially for me, where I could lay my head down to sleep at night. The memories are so vivid. I remember the linoleum floors, the wallpaper pattern, and the unique sound as the light switches were clicked on and off. Every detail that lingers in my mind brings memories of home. My grandparents put a lot of thought and preparation into my overnight stays with them to ensure I knew I was welcome and felt at home.

    19. Is there a certain place that means "home" to you?

John 14:1-4, "'Do not let your hearts be troubled. You believe in God, believe also in me. ² My Father's house has many rooms; if that were not so, would I have told you that I am going there to prepare a place for you?³ And if I go and prepare a place for you, I will come back and take you to be with me that you also may be where I am. ⁴ You know the way to the place where I am going.'"

From what John has recorded Jesus Himself as saying, not only are you welcomed into the Kingdom of God, but Jesus also has a place reserved with your name on it. Just as my grandparents prepared a place for me during my visits, Jesus has gone ahead into Heaven to prepare a place specifically for you. In this new home that He has prepared for you, you will get to be with Him forever.

    20. Have you ever considered that Jesus is preparing a special place in His Father's house just for you? What comfort does this bring you?

Heaven on Earth

Your earthly home may not be perfect; all of us who've spent any time on this earth have undoubtedly encountered pain, suffering, sin, tears, and mourning. But take heart and know that this will all pass away when Jesus brings His Heavenly Kingdom to earth. This world was never meant to completely satisfy. When God created us, He set Heaven upon our hearts. All our yearning will only be satisfied when we see Jesus face-to-face.

According to Scripture, at the appointed time—which only our heavenly Father knows—Jesus will return to earth to gather His loved ones to be with Him forever. And at that time, He will also renew the earth, not just back to its original grand beauty from during the time that Adam and Eve walked in the Garden of Eden, but a gloriously perfect beauty which surpasses anything we've previously seen or can comprehend with our finite minds. Our Lord and Savior will be at the focus and center of it all!

We have hope in our future, and Jesus calls us to persevere with that promised hope in mind—His hope does not disappoint. There is a great reward for those who love Him and are awaiting His return. He is going to make all things new; earth will no longer be tainted by sin and suffering. The earth will be remade into a dazzling, glorious sight. Safety will be found within the walls of God's Kingdom. We'll never have to lock our doors again because there will be no violence or fear. Love, peace, and joy will fill the air. Irritations and frustrations of this life will fade in light of what really matters—being with Jesus. Take heart, this heavenly hope is in your future.

There is no need for us to ever fear abandonment with our Lord. If He has promised to return for us, then He most certainly will.

1 Thessalonians 4:16-18, "For the Lord himself will come down from heaven, with a loud command, with the voice of the archangel and with the trumpet call of God, and the dead in Christ will rise first. ¹⁷ After that, we who are still alive and are left will be caught up together with them in the clouds to meet the Lord in the air. And so we will be with the Lord forever. ¹⁸ Therefore encourage one another with these words."

21. Please read the following verses for a glimpse into the extraordinary glory of your future home. Record your findings and thoughts on each.

- **Revelation 21:1-27**

- **Revelation 22:1-7**

- **Revelation 22:12-14**

22. Which words and phrases bring the greatest comfort to your heart?

23. Which descriptions of this beautiful city stand out most to you?

Reign

In God's Kingdom, as followers of Christ we will be given supreme liberty and honor. We will finally and perfectly enjoy the freedom that Jesus came to give us as the realization of our blessed position in Him comes to full fruition. We will reign with Jesus.

24. Please read the following verses to see this truth for yourself. Make note of the confirmations you find.

- **2 Timothy 2:11-13**

- **Revelation 5:9-11**

Crowns

What's a princess without a crown or tiara? God has crowned you with an imperishable crown which will grace your precious head forevermore. The crown that our Heavenly Father gives will last for all eternity. It won't bend or break, it won't get tarnished or lose a jewel, it can't be lost or stolen. His crown for you is eternal.

Proverbs 10:6, "Blessings crown the head of the righteous, but violence overwhelms the mouth of the wicked."

25. Please read the following verses to learn about the crown that God has in store for you. Record your findings on the various descriptions of His crown.

- **Psalm 8:3-6**

- **Psalm 103:1-5**

- **Psalm 149:4**

- **Isaiah 35:10**

- **1 Corinthians 9:24-25**

- **2 Timothy 4:8**

- **James 1:12**

- **1 Peter 5:4**

- **Revelation 2:10**

- **Revelation 3:11**

26. Which description of the crowns impacts you the most? Why?

Revelation 4:10-11, "They lay their crowns before the throne and say: 'You are worthy, our Lord and God, to receive glory and honor and power, for you created all things, and by your will they were created and have their being.'"

Our Glorified Bodies

Whatever ailments you are presently struggling against, know that they will not last forever. There is hope in the fact that the body you currently have will be gloriously transformed when Jesus returns. The body you live in now is meant for a temporary existence, topping off at around 100 years max. A heavenly, eternal Kingdom calls for a heavenly body that will last for all of eternity. I think of loved ones who've had great pain, handicaps, and diseases during their life on earth, and I have joy in knowing that God will bless them with new—not just restored, but completely new—bodies, that move with ease and freedom. Personally, I am looking forward to a day of no aching back, no pesky allergies, no reading glasses, and no orthotic inserts in my shoes. I also long for the day when my mind is renewed, and sin and temptation are no longer a struggle. There is perfect renewal in your future, and mine.

27. Read the following Scriptures and note what each says about the heavenly renewal of *you*.

- **Psalm 103:1-3**

- **1 Corinthians 15:50-58**

28. What aspect of a new heavenly body and mind are you most looking forward to?

Royal mindset

On a daily basis, worldly life swirls around us. Even though we are now a part of the Kingdom of God we remain living on the earth till Jesus calls us home, or until He returns for us. As we go about our daily routines, we need to keep our eyes firmly focused on the One who is ultimately in charge, the One who has given us a hope and a future, and the promise of everlasting life filled with goodness and excellence. Do not allow yourself to become overwhelmed by earthly life, but overcome by focusing on Jesus. Our perspective is different; we see the world through the truth of Jesus. We may not understand everything now, but someday Jesus will make it all clear by giving us a complete knowledge of Him and His ways.

29. Read the following verses and make note of the encouragement you find.

- **2 Corinthians 4:16-18**

- **1 Corinthians 13:12**

30. How can a royal mindset help you press on in your daily life?

Royal Servants

As with most things in the Kingdom of God, the idea of *who is greatest* is another which is flipped upside-down in contrast to the world. With Jesus as our supreme example, being ruler over all, having every reason to lord His position over everyone's head, He took the attitude of a servant. He laid down His place of honor to serve us. Jesus washed His disciple's feet; Jesus died on the cross for us. As His followers, our attitude is to be the same. As citizens in the Kingdom of God we aren't supposed to stand in a place of criticism and judgment over others, we are meant to stand in a place of servanthood, loving others into the Kingdom.

31. Read more on the attitude of servants in the following Scriptures. Make note of what you learn.

- **Mark 10:42-45**

- **Luke 22:24-30**

Ambassadors

Along with royal privileges we are given royal duties. As citizens who have been granted eternal security in the Kingdom of God we don't just get to sit around with our head in the clouds. We have responsibilities to tend to. Through Jesus, God has reconciled us to Himself. Now He has committed to us His message to share with others who are lost, lonely, hurting, weak, and scared. We have the greatest honor of all, representing Jesus to the world, and inviting others to be reconciled to God through Jesus, and into His Kingdom as well.

32. Read more about being an ambassador for God's Kingdom in the following verses and record your findings next to each.

- **2 Corinthians 5:14-21**

- **Romans 10:13-15**

The confidence that is found in being a child of God should cause the joy of the LORD to bubble up and burst forth from within us impacting the world around us!

Revelation 1:6, "and has made us to be a kingdom and priests to serve his God and Father—to him be glory and power for ever and ever! Amen."

As a result of writing this study my home is filled with crowns. Friends have abundantly blessed me with gifts of crowns in various forms, and I am so grateful. The very first gift I received was a necklace with the words "Daughter of the King" clearly written inside a glass bubble. I have been given a large antique crown—which was the centerpiece to a very grand and gorgeous flower arrangement—that now graces the coffee table as you enter my home. I have been blessed with a few pretty pictures of crowns. Sitting on my bathroom counter I have two beautiful boxes with crowns pictured on top—one is ivory-colored ceramic, and the other is a pink and gold paper hat box. A friend sewed me a lovely pillow, and made me two jars, all decorated with crowns and bees. One dear friend gifted me with a handmade cross-stitch, patterned with a crown and the words *I am loved, chosen, blessed, redeemed, adopted—A Daughter of the KING*. I have also been blessed to receive two more sparkly items that I can wear throughout the day as reminders of my identity: the first is a silver necklace with a dainty crown charm dangling from the chain (on the cover of this book); the second is a silver ring in the shape of a crown formed to surround my finger. All these crown gifts which are sprinkled throughout my home, serve as constant reminders of my true, royal identity as *A Daughter of the King*.

If you are prone to forgetting your royal identity, then I encourage you to find a crown or two and keep them in a place where you will see them every day. You can also get yourself a crown to put on every morning when you are brushing your teeth or getting ready to leave the house—just seeing yourself in the mirror with a crown on your head should remind you who you are so you can step out in confidence. It doesn't have to be fancy—it can be from a discount store, or you can even make a paper crown out of construction paper and tape, like one you may have made as a child.

At times, we each need a reminder of who we truly are—*A Daughter of the King.* Refer to God's Word and the special Scriptures that have spoken to your heart throughout this study often for a fresh boost of confidence as His child. Remember, you are loved, you are forgiven, you belong, you matter, you are beautiful, you have purpose, you are strong, and you my dear beloved sister-in-Christ, are royalty in the highest order!

The Simple Truth: You are Royalty!

A Simple Prayer: Dear Heavenly Father, thank You for all the blessings you continually pour into my life as Your beloved daughter. Help me to remember my royal position as I go about my daily life, and to be consciously aware of all the blessings that You have bestowed on me. Help me to keep my eyes, mind, and heart set on You and the eternal hope You give. Amen.

Time to Soar

As I was taking a walk one afternoon,
I looked up and saw a tremendous bird soaring high in the sky,
and the thought occurred to me that we too can soar to amazing heights
when we lay down our fears and insecurities,
and just believe God.
Disbelief is what keeps us tethered to the ground.
Jesus came to set us free.

Isaiah 40:31, "but those who hope in the LORD will renew their strength. They will soar on wings like eagles; they will run and not grow weary, they will walk and not be faint."

Ask Jesus to help you live in the reality of your freedom.
Ask Him to fill you with His Spirit to the point of overflowing.
Ask Him to reveal the enormity of His love to you.
Ask Him to give you eyes to see the hope of your future.

Ask Jesus to move your knowledge of Him from your head to your heart.
Ask Him to transform your life.
Ask Him to help you know Him more intimately.

He is able to do *abundantly more than you ask, or even imagine*. (Ephesians 3:20)

You are loved. You are forgiven and new. You belong. You matter.

You are beautiful. You have purpose. You are strong.

You are royalty in the Kingdom of God!

Leader Guide

Summary videos are found on YouTube: www.youtube.com/@beblessedandinspiredwithtracy/playlists

Introduction (study kick-off)

In case your group gets together before beginning the study, here are a couple ideas to get you started:

1. Grab a coffee, get comfy, open in prayer, and get to know each other. (These are your sisters-in-Christ and partners for the journey.)
2. Remind everyone that this is a safe place for sharing hearts and prayer requests. Everything must be kept confidential within the group. Try to stay on topic so everyone has time to share.
3. Have everyone introduce themselves and briefly share a little information—name, favorite food (mine is chips and salsa, chicken taco, rice and beans), hobby, or any other info you'd like to share.
4. What drew you to this study and what do you hope to gain from it?
5. Watch short *Introduction* video.

Lesson One—You are Loved

1. Open in prayer. Share overall impressions of the lesson—greatest takeaway and encouragement.
2. Discuss Jesus' encounter with *the woman at the well*.
3. From pages 7-8, discuss questions 2a, b, c, and d.
4. Have someone read Psalm 63:1-8 aloud (Page 8).
5. Discuss the verses from question 13 on page 12.
6. Turn to page 14 and share your answers relating to questions 17a, b, c, and d.
7. Watch video for *Lesson One* and then close by reading the *Simple Prayer* on page 16.

Lesson Two—You are Forgiven and New

1. Open in prayer. Share overall impressions of the lesson—greatest takeaway and encouragement.
2. To get things started, have someone read Romans 8:1 aloud.
3. Read Psalm 103:1-12 aloud and discuss all the benefits you discovered—question 6, page 23.
4. Regarding Jesus' interaction with the woman, discuss questions 7d, e, f, and g (pages 23-24).
5. Read Ephesians 4:22-24 aloud and share your thoughts about questions 8, 9, 10, and 11 (page 25).
6. How does Peter's do-over story encourage you?
7. Watch video summary of *Lesson Two* and then close by reading the *Simple Prayer* on page 32.

Lesson Three—You Belong

1. Open in prayer. Share overall impressions of the lesson—greatest takeaway and encouragement.
2. Discuss questions 2, 3, and 4 (page 35).
3. Read Ephesians 1:3-14 aloud and discuss questions 7 and 8 (page 37-38).
4. Turn to page 42 and discuss the verses from question 18 (page42).
5. Discuss question 21 and 22 (pages 43-44).
6. Watch a short video summary of *Lesson Three*, then close by reading the Simple Prayer (Page 47).

Lesson Four—You Matter

1. Open in prayer. Share overall impressions of the lesson—greatest takeaway and encouragement.
2. Read Matthew 10:29-31 aloud.
3. Discuss your observations regarding the story of Hagar. Look at questions 2 h, and i (page 50).
4. Dive into questions 3 f, g, and h (page 51).
5. Look at the verses from question 4, page 52. What assurance do you gain?
6. Reflect on question 11, page 59.
7. Watch a short video summary of *Lesson Four*, then close by reading the Simple Prayer (Page 60).

Lesson Five—You are Beautiful

1. Open in prayer. Share overall impressions of the lesson—greatest takeaway and encouragement.
2. Read Psalm 139:13-16 aloud and answer question 4 g (page 64).
3. Chat about question 6. (No judgement here.) Discuss question 7 too (page 65).
4. Discuss questions 9, 10, and 11 (page 67).
5. Read and review the verses from question 12 and share answers to question 13 (page 68).
6. Be brave and take a moment to brag on God's good creation—YOU. Share your answers to question 15. Don't be shy!
7. Watch a short video summary of *Lesson Five*, then close by reading the Simple Prayer (Page 71).

Lesson Six—You Have Purpose

1. Open in prayer. Share overall impressions of the lesson—greatest takeaway and encouragement.
2. Read Proverbs 20:5 aloud and share answers to questions 1 and 2 (page 72).
3. If you are comfortable, share your answers to questions 7, 8, 9, 10, 11, and 12.
4. Read 1 Corinthians 12:4-6 and answer question 16 (page 80).
5. Have someone read Colossians 3:17 aloud (from question 22, page 84).
6. Watch a short video summary of *Lesson Six*, then close by reading the Simple Prayer (Page 85).

Lesson Seven—You are Strong

1. Open in prayer. Share overall impressions of the lesson—greatest takeaway and encouragement.
2. Have everyone proclaim Philippians 4:13 together.
3. From page 89 read Ephesians 1:15-23 aloud and discuss questions 4 a, b, c, d, and e
4. Read 2 Peter 1:3 together and share your responses to questions 5, 6, and 7 (pages 90-91).
5. Discuss the Armor of God? Page 94, questions 9 a, b, c, d, e, and f.
6. Go over the verses from question 22 and share the authority you've been given (pages 98-99).
7. How do love, faith, hope, and joy help strengthen your spirit and resolve?
8. Watch short video summary of *Lesson Seven*, then close by reading the Simple Prayer (Page 103).

Lesson Eight—You are Royalty

1. Open in prayer. Share overall impressions of the lesson—greatest takeaway and encouragement.
2. Read Revelation 17:14 aloud, and discuss the verses found in question 1 (page 105).
3. How has your understanding of the Beatitudes changed?
4. Discuss the following sections: *Heaven on Earth, Crowns, Our Glorified Bodies,* and *Ambassadors*.
5. Watch a short video summary of *Lesson Eight*, then close by reading the Simple Prayer (Page 121).

A Special Thanks

To my fellow sojourners at Club 31, for continually encouraging and supporting me, for your dedication to the Word of God, and for your treasured input on this study.

To the women of Teen Challenge, your lives are a shining example of what it means to sit at Jesus' feet and live wholly focused on the Lord.

Russell, Camden, and Christian, I am so grateful for your love and support throughout this journey.

To Camden for your cover designs, and invaluable creative expertise.

To Christian for your knowledgeable writing guidance.

Thank you, Stella, for being my sweet inspiration.

Thank you, Melanie Prieger, for your editing skills, and your attention to detail.

A special thank you to Grandma and Grandpa Leavitt for teaching me about Jesus.

Most of all, I offer my gratitude to the Lord for allowing me to share this message with you.

Getting to Know the Author

First and foremost, I am a woman who loves the Lord with all her heart; I can't imagine doing life without Him. I am married to a wonderful man, and I'm a mother of two grown men (who used to be little boys). I am a daughter, a sister, a friend, a neighbor. I spend much of my time writing Bible studies, devotionals, freelance articles, and my weekly blog. I write to inspire others to deepen their relationships with Jesus through the study of His Word. A great passion of mine is serving in women's ministry and teaching others about the hope, joy, peace, and confidence that is rightfully theirs as a child of God. I enjoy taking walks outside and enjoy traveling and taking pictures (the photos on my book covers are taken by me). Although I find delight in all flowers, roses are my favorite fragrant blooms.

I'm so happy to have you join me on this journey and hope that you find some encouragement as we walk with the Lord together.

Website: www.beblessedandinspired.com

YouTube Videos: www.youtube.com/@beblessedandinspiredwithtracy/playlists

Spotify Podcast: Be Blessed and Inspired with Tracy Hill

Blog: tracyhillbeblessed.substack.com

My Books: amazon.com/author/beblessedandinspired

Esty Shop: BeBlessedandInspired - Etsy

Website Videos Podcast Blog Etsy

Additional Inspiration

Available at Amazon.com

Colossians: Set Your Heart on Things Above (A Bible Study)—We will experience a glorious shift in our perspective by meditating on the supremacy of Christ and on our fullness in Him. Our relationships will be greatly impacted for the better. The peace, hope, and joy of Christ will help us overcome and persevere.

Come to the Father: Drawing Near to God Through Prayer and Scripture (A Devotional and Prayer Journal)— Every good relationship requires open and consistent communication and our relationship with God is no different. We will learn to pray daily with Scripture as our guide—approaching God in both spirit and truth. My hope is that we grow more confident and comfortable in talking to God on a consistent basis.

Worship and Wonder: Faith-Filled Devotions—Throughout this devotional, you and I will meditate on God's Word. Every page is filled with inspiration meant to remind us of our blessings, fill us with hope, and grow our faith.

Promise and Possibilities: Hope-Filled Devotions—You will glimpse the promise that life holds and the possibility of all that can be when you place your hope in Jesus. He is truly the One who holds the key."

Confidence and Crowns: Devotions for A Daughter of the King—The devotions, stories, and Scripture you will encounter, are all intended to point you to the reality of who you are in God's eyes. It is time to put aside your doubts and insecurities and live a life of confidence.

Lilies and Lemonade: Joy-Filled Devotions—*Lilies and Lemonade* represents two philosophies which hold the key to optimistic living. A joy-filled perspective is available to us when we look at life with the proper Jesus-filled mindset.

Matthew: Your Kingdom Come (A Bible Study)—By studying this amazing Gospel, we will come to know Jesus better and, as a result, fall even more deeply in love with Him. We will hear His teachings, witness His miracles, see His power, and feel His love.

Endorsements

In *A Daughter of the King: Gaining confidence as a child of God* author Tracy Hill provides a thorough, clear, and compelling look at every believer's identity in Christ. This study will specifically help women discover their beauty, identity, and value as a daughter of their Heavenly Father. Whether used for individual or group study, *A Daughter of the King* stands out as a biblical and practical resource that God will use to empower women to live and love like Jesus confidently more and more every day!

—Shawn Thornton, Senior Pastor, Calvary Community Church,
Westlake Village, CA

This is a Bible study that would benefit any young girl or woman interested in finding her way to the riches and promises of what God has for her in His Kingdom. Tracy has done an excellent job in each chapter of simply yet concisely showing the reader/student how to grow in Christ each and every day by applying the truths she has put together from Scripture. Well done!

—Rita Warren, Board Chair Communitas International,
(formerly Christian Associates International)

For over 30 years I've been working with women who struggle with their identity. Their freedom comes when they know who they are in Christ. This book is one of the best complete studies I've had the privilege of reading.

—Rosie Weir, Director of Tri-County Teen Challenge

A Daughter of the King is a beautiful study that reminds women who they are and whose they are. It brings scripture to life with vivid stories, engaging questions and a call to dig in. If you want to know how to live in the fullness of a life with Christ, A Daughter of the King is the perfect study for you.

—Amy Pendergraft, Director of Women and Family Ministries,
Calvary Church of Pacific Palisades

Tracy Hill has written a wonderful study that reminds us to stand firm in God's love and truth, knowing who He has created us to be—*A Daughter of the King* in the midst of a world that tells us differently. You will be greatly blessed by this study.

—Christine Matsuura, Women's Bible Study Leader

Who am I? Is your soul thirsty? *A Daughter of the King* is a heartfelt journey which seeks to satisfy these questions by confidently sharing scriptures of God's love, forgiveness, acceptance, purpose, and strength. Tracy's inspirational thoughts and stories enhance scripture in showing how much you matter to God and how beautiful you are in His eyes! Quench your soul and know you are a daughter of the King.

—Tori Bellino

Tracy Hill's study is a celebration of the amazingly powerful love of God. It directly addresses the feelings of insecurity, doubt, and fear that plague so many women today. Based firmly in God's Word, the biblical truths of our spiritual inheritance as *daughters* unfolds with each chapter, helping us to begin to fully understand the hope, confidence, and purpose we can embrace when we belong to Christ. As the parent of a grown daughter, a professional who has counseled with women and teens, and a woman with my own personal struggles of insecurity and doubt, the *Daughter* Study is an important, comprehensive, and refreshing teaching, beneficial for women of any age.

—Judy Kerner

A Daughter of the King Bible Study was truly a blessing to me. Tracy's love for Jesus was evident in every detail. Each day as I sat to do homework, I felt like I was sitting with a friend and sharing my heart. God's Word, along with Tracy's personal stories and experiences, provided a clarity that helped me grow in my knowledge. It related to my everyday life in such a way that the message was sealed on my heart, and I felt comfortable sharing with others what I had learned. Don't miss the opportunity to dive into this study. I promise you, God will reveal himself in a way that is life-changing!

—Donna Severn

A Daughter of the King has inspired me and taught me so much about being a woman of God! I know for sure that I am loved, forgiven, and special, and that God has a plan and a purpose for me here above all earthly things. This study brought me to my knees and raised me up again as a confident, loved woman of God! Thank you, Tracy, for the time and love you put into this study. I pray that many others will be as touched by it as I have been!

—Susan Brewer

Dr. Henrietta Mears once wrote, "You teach a little by what you say. You teach the most by what you are." Tracy Hill certainly lives out this great truth. *A Daughter of the King* is focused on Christ and His Gospel message, and will help all who read it to become genuine disciples who actually walk the talk as they realize their precious identity.

—Beverley Carter

If you have never struggled with insecurity, yearned to be loved & accepted, or felt like you couldn't live up to God's expectations, this book is not for you. But if you, like me, ever find yourself dealing with those things, let Tracy's words and the Scripture underlying them whisper words of truth into your soul. You truly are *A Daughter of the King*, and this book will help you live out your royal position with confidence!

—Melanie Prieger

www.ingramcontent.com/pod-product-compliance
Lightning Source LLC
Chambersburg PA
CBHW050455110426
42743CB00017B/3364